THE TEMPLE IN THE HEART

★

THE TEMPLE IN THE HEART

★

Rev. JAMES REID, D.D.

ABINGDON-COKESBURY PRESS

New York • Nashville

THE TEMPLE IN THE HEART
COPYRIGHT, MCMXXXVIII
BY WHITMORE & SMITH

CONTENTS

★

CONTENTS

CONTENTS

CONTENTS

I

THE TEMPLE IN THE HEART

*"The true worshipers shall worship
the Father in spirit and in truth."*
JOHN 4: 23

SOME of Christ's greatest words were spoken to the most unlikely people. Among these is his saying about worship. It was spoken to a woman of loose life in a casual talk beside a well. He and she had come to that point in their talk where God is heard knocking at the door. We cannot be long in the presence of Christ without hearing that knock. The woman tried to switch the conversation off into a religious discussion. That is a frequent method of evasion. Which is the place where one ought to worship? she asked. This gave Christ his opportunity. He refused to be headed off. The true place of worship is not a geographical locality. It is not a special place at all. God is not localized in any particular spot or building. It is in the temple within the heart that we must find him. There we must worship him in spirit and in reality.

John Ruskin points this out in one of his penetrating comments. "I have seen over the doorway of many a church the words carved, 'This is the

11

house of God.' " He bids us note where these words were first spoken. They were uttered by Jacob one morning on the moorland on awaking from the dream in which he had seen the ladder and the angels. It was a bare spot, wind-swept and torrent-bitten: but he met God there. The conclusion is that God's house is not a particular building, but "any place where God lets down his ladder." That is useful to remember when we are thinking of how worship can become a reality. It is not the place, but the spirit within, that makes worship real. The place where we worship may be a barn or a cathedral. It may be a quiet nook in the garden or among the hills. It may even be in some dreary workshop amid the whir of machines, or where Brother Lawrence worshiped, in the kitchen among the pots and pans. God comes to dwell in the temple of the heart, and there we worship him.

But what is worship? How can we make it a reality? These are questions that need to be asked. The worship of God is the surrender of our whole being in adoration and consecration to God. It is the act of opening up heart and mind to his goodness and love, so that he takes first place in our souls. It is offering to him the central place within. For we all have this temple within. Every man carries in his soul a secret place where he keeps the things that are sacred. We all reverence something. The real disaster is not the lack of worship. It is that we

12

often worship the wrong things. The inner shrine is tenanted by some idol to which we give our devotion, and which has the power to mold our actions and shape our lives. We may bow down in church with every appearance of devotion. We may even think with reverence and adoration of God. But all the time what is holding the central place in our hearts may be something very different. It may, for instance, be money or the things that money can buy. Money has a tremendous power over our hearts if we give it a chance. It can fill the inner shrine with its fascination. It offers so many glittering things to those who have it. It was this which made Christ warn us that it is difficult for them that have riches to enter the Kingdom of God. It made Wesley say that when he had any money, he got rid of it as quickly as possible lest it should find a way into his heart.

Other things also may fill this inner shrine. Success may do it, if we put success first in life. Power may do it. The power to dominate the lives of others can become a fanatical object of worship. It is that which inspires most dictators, though some who are doing service to others are not free from it. The effort to help others may easily become the subtle satisfaction of a sense of power. Or again the image that fills that inner shrine may be an inflated picture of ourselves. We may value most of all in life our own reputation, our own comfort. We may

13

have such a highly colored picture of our own virtues that we think we can do no wrong. It amounts to the worship of ourselves.

The truth is that we really worship what we value most. That which decides our actions and shapes our desires and ambitions is the true object of our worship. Mr. Gandhi made a comment about us that ought to make us examine ourselves. He said that while we professed to worship a crucified Christ, our real gods are wealth and power.

If religion is to be real, we must examine our hearts to find out what we value most. We must let God fill His temple within us. We must make sure, also, that it is the true God we worship. He must be no longer a Being to fear. Nothing has done more to turn people from God than the confusion between fear and awe. Christ came to banish the sense of fear. His name for God was always, "Father." It is a father's face that must fill the inner shrine. When that happens, the sense of awe will make us hold our breath and bow the knee. Who can look at the sorrow and love that made Christ's crown at Calvary without the most soul-searching awe? But confidence will be there also, and love, and "a wonderful sort of gladness."

This inner experience is the true effect of the act of worship. We shall go out from it with our values changed. The idols will be dethroned. We shall value goodness more than money. We shall value

14

character more than success. We shall desire to be of service to others and not to have power for ourselves.

But how can our worship become real? How can we come to adore the goodness and love of God? We cannot love to order. We cannot even admire a picture by making up our minds to do so. We can, however, look at the picture with open minds and a willingness to have its beauty lay hold of our hearts. This also we can do with God as we see Him in Christ. We can come to Him with hearts willing to be won. We can bring the lamp of our devotion ready to be lit by His flame. That is the value of the act of worship and of a special place of worship. They help us into the mood in which the door in the heart can open and God can come to His temple within.

II

THE TEST OF SONSHIP

"When we cry, 'Abba, Father,' the
Spirit testifieth with our spirit
that we are the sons of God."
(MOFFATT) ROM. 8: 15

THERE is a popular idea that all men are the sons of
God. That is not the teaching of the New Testament.
God is always Father, and the Father of all. He
loves and cares for us all. That is His constant
attitude. But we do not become His sons in reality
till we have the spirit and attitude of sons. It is the
heart and the will that count in this matter. There
are sons in the flesh who are not sons in the spirit.
They care nothing for home or parents. They are
not really sons. The prodigal was in that position
when he flung away from home and rioted in a far
country. He had no love or care for his father then.
But when love awoke in him amid the ruins of his
burnt-out life, and he set out for home with the cry,
"Father," in his heart, he had begun to be a son.
When he got home in this new spirit of trust and
obedience, the father spoke the truth about it. "This
my son was dead, and is alive again; he was lost, and
is found." There is a point at which we become the
sons of God. It is there our true life begins.

16

What is the test of our sonship? The big test, of course, is our life. We show our spirit in the way we live. They who are guided by the Spirit of God are the sons of God. But there is another test. "When we cry, 'Abba, Father,' the Spirit testifieth with our spirit that we are the sons of God."

How do we think of God? How do we feel toward Him? Are we afraid of Him? Do we think of Him as some vague, stern, but kindly Being, beyond our range? Is He just a somewhat forbidding Stranger who invades our life disturbingly at times when conscience jogs us? Or do we think of Him as Father? When our minds turn to Him in thought or prayer, do our hearts rest in quiet confident love upon Him, as children with a father whom they fully trust and love? That is the test.

When we think of this feeling toward God as Father we find there are various elements in it. For one thing it means that God has become intimate and personal to us. He has ceased to stand on the threshold and has become a living, loving Reality to us. We become conscious of things we can only explain as His touch or His voice. There is a sense of perfect understanding. The shadows of fear or of guilt are gone. A well-known scholar long ago had a prayer that he prayed morning and evening. He just said to God, "Things still stand between us on the old terms." Whatever the day had brought, there was no estrangement between him and God.

17

He rested in a love that was infinitely understanding and utterly forgiving. The word "Father" means all that.

To call God "Father" in reality means also perfect trust in His care for us. It means to believe in His care as something definite and real. He can help us in all our daily concerns. He is interested in the things that make up our life. In the United States they have a happy way of speaking about "taking care" of one. The hotel manager says he will "take care" of you. The man who arranges your tickets describes himself as "taking care" of you. It sounds very personal and feels very comforting. To trust the Father means that He takes care of us. He thinks about the details of our life, the struggle to make ends meet, the sick child at home, the things that worry us in business. He answers prayer. We are apt to think of the world as a big, soulless machine that has no room in it for God to intervene on our behalf. So we battle and struggle on alone, with God shut out. It is a simpler and more child-like faith that Jesus offers us. "Your Father knoweth." He calls us to a big faith that relies on God in everything.

But to know God as Father means the spirit that is also ready to say, "Brother." "Love your enemies," Jesus said, "that ye may be the children of your Father." It is not easy to believe that God cares as much about other people as He does about

18

ourselves. It is sometimes rather a shock to our self-esteem to realize it. But that is what His Fatherhood means. He thinks about the people we dislike. He loves the stupid and the wretched and the sinful. The people we call foreigners are also His children. They all belong to His family, though they may not have come to take their place in it. Some of them have had the door of the Father's house shut in their faces, and only the hand of love can reopen it. There are many to whom the Father can only be introduced by those who are truly their brothers. But to say "Father" sincerely means that the spirit of the home is in us; and that enables us to see others as our brothers.

How do we get this spirit of sonship? The only way is to see God as Father. Only that will awaken it and draw out our trust and obedience. Philip was right when he said, "Show us the Father, and it sufficeth us." If we can see God like that, we can trust Him through everything. We may not be able to understand, but peace will come into the heart even in the darkest day if we can look into the darkness and say, "Father."

There is only one way to find this child-spirit toward God. It is to see Him reflected in Christ. For he came to introduce us to God the Father. That is the only way in which the incredible truth of God's Fatherhood can come to us. We go to Christ with our thought of God dim and darkened with fears and doubts. We find that God is no stranger, but a Friend whose love seeks us in Christ. His hand is stretched out in the hand of Christ to open the gates of His own fellowship. As we let Christ lead us, the word "Father" awakes in our hearts. There is no other Name that will describe all we feel about God when we see Him in Jesus. As we whisper that Name to God in perfect trust we are on the way home. We have begun to be the sons of God.

III

A WHOLE-TIME RELIGION

"With part thereof he roasted flesh,
with part he warmeth himself; and
the residue thereof he maketh a god."
Isa. 44: 16, 17

THERE is plenty of humor to be found in the Bible.
Isaiah's description of the idol maker is full of it.
It might well laugh idolatry out of existence. It pictures an idol worshiper at work. He cuts down a
tree. Part of it he uses to make a fire to warm himself. Part of it he uses to roast his food. Then,
being warmed and fed, he sees the remnant and be-
takes himself to making out of it the image of a god.
To this he bows down, saying, "Deliver me; for
thou art my god."

Translate this into modern terms, and we have a
living picture of the place which religion holds in the
life of many people. We parcel out our time—so
much for business, so much for pleasure, so much for
worship and prayer. That is a perfectly right thing
to do. Life is not properly balanced if any of its
big interests are left out. Whatever else we leave
out we must find a place for religion. A traveler
tells how in an American hotel he found a plan of
the city with all the principal places of interest
marked and the way to get to them. It showed

21

theaters, cinemas, libraries, post office, railway station, but the churches were left out. The hotel advertisement said that it was "Nearest to Everything," but could it be everything with religion left out? When we apportion our time we must make room for that. We should apportion our money in the same way. If we are careful in its management, we use so much for food, so much for pleasure, so much for religion and philanthropy. If we are wise, also, we apportion our thinking. The mind should not always be traveling in one groove. We have to think of business most of the time, but we should find time for reading. We should find time, too, to think of God and the meaning of life. But how easily the part we give to religion begins to shrink. It often depends on how much time is left over when pleasure and business have had their share. "The residue he maketh a god." After we have warmed and fed ourselves, the rest we devote to God. After we have spent the whole day in other interests, till mind and strength are gone, there may be five odd minutes for prayer. After a busy week, Sunday worship will have to take its chance of whether or not we feel inclined for it. Many people decide the question of Sunday worship by the strength they have over after the hectic pleasure of the evening before. "The residue he maketh a god." It is the same with giving. How much of our giving is calculated and proportioned? How often is it dependent on what we have

22

left over, when the other things have had their full share? It is the same with thinking. A man will spend hours over a chess problem or a bridge problem, who will not give five minutes to the problem of his own moral life or his right relationships with others.

This opens up a very difficult question for some of us. The struggle of life is hard. It is not easy to satisfy the needs of the body. Food and shelter are grim necessities and the most of life is taken up with getting these. Religion is crowded out by the pressure of life. Is it to be wondered that some people begin to ask if religion is a necessity? Is it not just a luxury, to be enjoyed by people with an ample margin both of time and means?

But this way of thinking of religion, as a special department of life, is all wrong. There was one interesting thing about this savage. Religion was one of his big needs. It was as essential as food and shelter. It had a place. But what is its place? Religion is not merely one of the needs of life. It is an attitude to God that we must take all through our life. This man should have practiced his religion in the way he cut his tree and made his fire. Not on one day only or at one special time of the day, but every day and all the time—that is the place of religion. It is a whole-time business or it is nothing. It is a daily, hourly consecration. It is a continuous way of life, a constant fellowship with God. Religion demands all our activities. It comes to shape the spirit of all the work and struggle and enjoyment of life. It is not an addition to the things we do, but a way of doing everything. It is not setting apart a bit of time for God. It means the whole of life tuned to the spirit of devotion.

There is nothing that is exempt from the religious spirit. Nothing is to be kept out of our fellowship with God. The life in the home must be inspired by our devotion to Him. His love must be the keystone of all our loving. The work of the shop or the office or the house must be lifted into the service of God. His purpose must guide and fashion all our ambitions. Even our pleasures must be enjoyed in fellowship with God. If there is any pleasure in which we cannot feel that He is with us, there is something wrong with it. The use of all our gifts must be directed by His Spirit. "That woman sings to God," said a friend to me once, as we listened to a fine singer.

That was part of the service Christ did for religion. He took it out into the open. He set it working in the home. He brought it into all his relationships with people. All his contacts with men and women were the channel of the love of God that burned in his heart. He came to show us that secret, and to enable us to practice that technique of living. The whole of life is the field for religion. The whole world is the temple of our worship.

24

But this does not mean that no special time need be set apart for definite communion with God. Some people, taking this broad view, may ask the question:

> Where's the need of temple
> When the walls of the world are that?

The truth can be made plain by a simple illustration. If a violin is to produce true music, it must be constantly retuned. Worship and prayer are the means of retuning our minds and spirits to the will of God. It is true that some people make worship an end in itself. They speak of doing their duty to God. They do not realize that the real meaning of worship is to bring us into the spirit in which life is to be lived all through. To be content with worship without seeking to live out our faith is like tuning a violin without attempting to play a tune. But to try to play the violin without retuning it means that the strings become limp and useless. The same kind of thing happens with our souls when worship is left out and no time is set apart for making touch with God. The strings of faith and devotion will produce no music of Christian living. The man who knows what a glorious thing real religion is will want to renew from day to day his touch with God. He will want time to shake off the grip of the world with its fear and its seduction. He will seek a special time to be alone with God that he may find the power to give it all to Him.

25

IV

DEEDS AND DEVOTION

"Why call ye me, Lord, Lord, and
do not the things which I say?"
LUKE 6: 46

THE way to reality in religion is to put Christ first.
It is found when we call him "Lord," and make his
will and purpose ours. When the Roman official
mentioned the early Christians in his report to head-
quarters, he said that they were people who met together "to sing hymns to Christ as God."

But that is only the starting point of real religion.
It is the keynote of the march. We must walk the
road. We must do the things Christ asks. Devotion
to Christ is the secret of power. It kindles emotion,
and all emotion is power. Emotion is that which
produces movement. The love of Christ is the
strongest force in the world. It has made heroes.
It has moved men and women to incredible deeds of
sacrifice. It has started world movements. One
thinks of Livingstone, plodding through the African
jungle, making roads in it for Christ with every
step. What kept him going on? It was the power
created in him by devotion to Christ. For, as he
went through "the lone, lone wilderness," he tells us
that he sang to himself the old hymn:

26

Jesus, the very thought of Thee
With sweetness fills my breast.

But that power needs to be set to work if religion is to be real. This is where unreality often creeps in. Christ found it so in his own day. "Why call ye me, Lord, Lord, and do not the things which I say?"

There are temptations in this devotion. It may become a substitute for action. We may content ourselves with feeling, instead of doing. We may be satisfied with the mere thrill of devotion. We talk of "enjoying" a religious service. It is good that we should do so. There is joy in having courage restored, faith quickened, and truth made clear. The feeling awakened in a religious gathering may be the purest joy known to man. To be in touch with God "puts gladness in the heart," as the Psalmist said, "more than when corn and wine increase." But that gathered emotion is very much like raising steam in an engine boiler. It cannot be an end in itself. It must be put to work if it is not to become an unreality. The temptation is to make this inner feeling take the place of action. We may confuse approval of the truth with obedience to it. As Miss Underhill says, it is "like reading a book on engineering instead of getting to work, putting on overalls, doing the job." What ought to be inspiration for service becomes an emotional luxury.

There is another and more subtle danger. We may make devotion a means of evading the ways of

27

duty. We may use our adoration of Christ as a means of avoiding his challenge. Mr. Bernard Shaw accuses us of what he calls the "idolatrous worship" of Christ. We give him, he says, the same admiration as we give to a statue or picture. We thus prevent him stepping down from his pedestal, or walking out of the picture and commanding our obedience. Many people think of him as a sublime Figure, "not as One who is real, who means what he says, a force like electricity, only waiting the requisite machinery to come into our lives with the revolutionary effect." There is a good deal of truth in this charge. What does it mean to call Christ divine? It means to say that he is right when he speaks about the way to live, about prayer, about forgiveness, about peace. It means that he has the right to command obedience, and that his way is the only way in which life can be truly lived. But we may think that to call him "Lord" is all that he asks and all that is required of us. His word is a cold douche for this unreal devotion. It is common sense. Why call him "Master," if we do not, in fact, obey him?

Of course, the Christian life is not merely doing Christian things with conscious purpose. It is a Christian way of doing everything. It is a new spirit that flows through all we do. The finest product of Christ's Spirit in our lives is a quality, an influence of which we may be quite unconscious. This is one result of devotion. As we open our hearts to his loveliness, something of his beauty passes into our mind and spirit. It influences our actions, our speech, our feeling toward others. "The grace of our Lord Jesus Christ be with you." The best description of grace is what may be called charm—the effortless self-forgetfulness of love. That is a real part of the Christian benediction.

But we must not rely on this unconscious influence. The true artist reflects in his picture the beauty which he is looking at. It passes through his brush on to his canvas. Without that he would be no artist. But he has to make an effort to set down what he sees, and to work out his vision of beauty. He must strive to be faithful. He must use all his energy and skill to put his emotion into paint, to make it actual. We also must make efforts if our religion is to be real. We must do what Christ asks. We must find out what he wants us to do in the home, the office, the world. That is how religion becomes real. We may feel the beauty of the forgiving spirit. But what of the actual person who needs our forgiveness? Is there someone to whom we ought to speak or write? We may feel the glow of the unselfish spirit. But is there someone by our side who needs personal help—it may be at a cost of time and money?

When we let Christ come down from the pedestal into our life—into our home or our office—he will ask of us very definite things. Till we obey him there, our devotion is only a sentiment. It has not

29

become a living power. God's way into His world
through us is blocked at that point. Our own religion will remain unreal. Feeling will never deepen
into conviction. If the devotion kindled in all the
churches on any Sunday were put into definite deeds
on Monday, the new world would begin to appear.
This also would happen: the low mist of doubt and
depression that often hangs around faith would begin
to lift. The way of definite, costly obedience is the
way of illumination. "If any man will do his will,"
said Christ, "he shall know."

V

IS OUR RELIGION AN ESCAPE?

"O that I had wings like a dove! for
then would I fly away, and be at rest."
Ps. 55: 6

THAT is not the language of aspiration. It is a cry
for escape. It is the craving for some retreat from
the struggles and burdens of life. We are all
tempted at times to seek such an escape. The burdens of life press so heavily that we desire to get
away from them. Life offers us many methods of
escape. Some people seek it in amusement; some in
drugs which soothe the brain and calm their jagged
nerves. Some seek escape in things which are good,
in books or music or work. Poets have found escape
from an unhappy home or a defeated life by writing
lovely verses. Others even seek escape in working
feverishly for their fellows. Service may be the
effort to escape from our own problems, or from the
hardness of our lot, by trying to solve the problems
of other people or to ease their load.

Religion may also offer us the means of escape.
That is the charge which has been thrown at it by
some ardent socialists. Karl Marx called religion
"the opiate of the people." His charge was that it

31

taught people to be resigned to their conditions instead of fighting against them. It is an anodyne against the discontent which, in his view, is the only source of social progress and of revolutionary change. But he is not the only one who has made this charge against religion. There are those who tell us that our belief in God is merely the projection of our unsatisfied desires upon an empty sky. The longing for dependence on God is merely the craving of the child to get back to the shelter of the mother's arms, in face of a cold and hostile world. The honest way, in this view, is to be done with religion and face life without anesthetics.

It must be confessed that these charges have often been true. Religion can be used to dull us into contentment with conditions that ought to be changed. We can be resigned to things as the Mohammedan is resigned to fate. We can take things as the will of God which are not His will for us or for other people. I remember an old lady who refused to have any help in cleaning up a dirty room in which she lived. Her one reply was, "I shall have a mansion some day." Instead of meeting her troubles, she found escape from them in the thought of heaven beyond. She longed for the day when she would fly away and be at rest.

Are there not some of us who make our approval of the ideal in life an excuse for doing nothing to put it into practice? It is so delightful to picture to ourselves the ideal life and to dream dreams of the kind of world which Christ could make it and in those dreams to fly away on the wings of imagination and be at rest. It is so easy to retreat into the thought of the love of God when we should be facing the hard tasks of life. We may mistake the luxury of feeling good, which a religious service may bring, for the way of doing good. Religion can be a retreat from life. It can be a form of escape from a situation which is not easy to face. Even the blessed fact of God's forgiveness may be a shelter from His light. We may seek escape from the claim of conscience in the thought of the kindly Fatherhood of God, like a child who shelters from the shame of disobedience in the indulgence of his father. Is our religion an escape?

But what of the promises of the Bible? What of the words of Christ himself, "Come unto me, and I will give you rest"? Is not prayer of necessity a retreat from the world? Surely that is part of its value for us. We close the door upon the things that worry and annoy, and find in God's fellowship an inner peace which the world cannot give. From that renewal of our dependence on Him we come forth refreshed. We are able to look life in the face, and to see the things that trouble us in their true perspective. The astronomer uses a long telescope in an observatory tower. Part of its purpose is to shut out all other light, that he may gaze on the star which he is studying. Must we not escape from the world and its throng and pressure, in order to find an undimmed vision of things eternal? Must we not seek the silence, that the Voice within may have a chance to be heard?

It is true that Christ offers us rest. But what kind of rest? It is not escape from the world and its cares into his love. It is the rest that comes from finding in him the will of God, and coming into union with it. It is the rest that comes from taking our burdens from him, and facing them in his strength. "Take my yoke upon you," he said. A yoke is not an escape from a burden. It is that which binds us to a burden. His yoke is not relief from trouble. It is the gift of a new attitude to our burdens, and a new spirit in which to bear them. Things worry and fret our souls only because we have no resources with which to meet them. They weigh us down because we have no power to stand upright under the load. It is this power which Christ gives.

But he never meant his rest to be an escape from life. His own prayer life was not a flight from the world. It was not an escape from the storm. It was the secret of peace within the storm. He knew God's call in the sting of difficulty, and in the weight of the burdens he had to carry. He heard the whisper of God's love in the impulse that led him to face the Cross. He was tempted at the last to seek some escape from it. But he could not keep his peace

34

except in taking it and bearing it with all his heart.
Even on the Cross he refused the anodyne they
offered him to dull his mind and soothe his pain.
That is his way for us in face of the troubles of life.
It is to meet them without shrinking or evasion.
When we think of him, we are shamed out of our
weakness and fear. Fellowship with him can never
be a coward's castle.

> Jesus, whose lot with us was cast,
> Who saw it out from first to last,
> I would not to Thy bosom fly
> To hide me till the storms go by.

He can give us the spirit in which to meet anything
that comes, and stand up to it. And when we face it
in his strength, the center of the storm becomes the
place of deeper fellowship with him.

VI

HOW GOD GETS THROUGH

*"I have seen thy face, as though
I had seen the face of God."*
Gen. 33 : 10

No greater tribute than this could be paid by one man to another. The strange thing is that it was paid by a religious man to a brother who was not religious. For Jacob, with all his ugly faults, was a religious man. Esau, his brother, was a pagan. The writer to the Hebrews calls him "a profane person," which means that he had no sacred place in his heart. He was once so hungry that he sold his right to be the head of the family for a dish of lentils. He was a rough, lusty man of the desert. Yet it was of this man that Jacob said, "I have seen thy face, as though I had seen the face of God."

What made him feel this and say it? One night Jacob had an experience that changed his life, and turned him from being a rather shady business man into a humble servant of God. He was on his way to the old home with his family and his wealth, after many years of exile. But he was afraid to meet Esau, whom years before he had tricked. He made the best plans he could, and sent on ahead some valuable presents for his brother. But the night before the meeting his conscience awoke. God spoke to him and convinced him of the shame and sordidness of the wrong he had done his brother. He was brought to a sense of sin. He had never realized this before, and he was crushed and broken by it. Full of this new shame and the old fear, he set out to meet Esau. But Esau ran and fell on his neck and kissed him. It reminds us of the home-coming of the prodigal in Christ's story. The old estrangement vanished. The wrong had been for-given. But with Esau's forgiveness there came to Jacob the sense of God's forgiveness. The love of God broke out on that rugged weather-beaten face like sunlight through a thundercloud. And Jacob burst out, "I have seen thy face, as though I had seen the face of God."

This brings to our mind the fact that God is made real to people by people. Nature can do something to reveal Him. But nature has no heart. God can speak to us in flowers only when we know that it is He who speaks. It needs a human heart to reveal Him fully. In the Bible God speaks as in no other book. But even there it is through men that He speaks. It is through what men have felt and said and done and been. This is seen most of all in the fact that He sent Christ, a Man like ourselves. He showed us "His glory in the face of Jesus Christ." Only thus could He show us His very self.

It is very comforting to think what this means. God can best be known to us through a Man, One who worked as a carpenter, who went in and out of humble homes and took little children on his knee. We might almost call it the homeliness of God. In all that is best in us He is like ourselves. That is indeed what Christ said. He told us to picture God in the light of what is best in ourselves, and we would be right.

But this means that it is by people such as us that God gets through to others. For He is love, and love can only come home to us through people who love. There are many to whom God is not real because they have never known anyone who really cared for them. If we know God, on the other hand, we can generally trace the experience to someone in whose love and care God became real. Most of us can think of one at least of whom we can say, "I have seen thy face, as though I had seen the face of God."

It is a startling thing to realize this. Our treatment of others may be helping or hindering their experience of God. It ought to make us very careful. It should keep us living near to Christ where the spirit of love can be learned. We are always meeting people whose hearts are ready for the healing or the comforting that can make God's love real.

But the surest way is in our forgiveness. It was in Esau's forgiveness that God got through to Jacob. Our forgiveness of others has more power to manifest God than anything else we do. For when we forgive, love is victorious in us over the spirit of evil. In that forgiving love God's grace shines through.

The diary of the Japanese criminal who was called "A Gentleman in Prison" makes this clear. He had been given a New Testament, and one night took it up to read it. He opened it at the Sermon on the Mount, but was not deeply touched. Later, he began to read the story of the trial and crucifixion of Christ. When he read how Christ on the Cross prayed for his enemies, he said he felt "his heart stabbed as if by a five-inch nail." Here is One being slain though he is innocent, and by those he had tried to help. And on his Cross he prays for them. This can be no other than God. So he reasoned. But it was more than reasoning. The divine love released in that forgiving spirit of Christ had found him and won him. He saw in the face of the Crucified the face of God.

Can God's forgiveness ever really get through to people unless we forgive them? It is very doubtful if it can. This is the true absolution—our forgiveness of those who have wronged us, our friendship with those who have sinned. That is what we often forget. There are people who cannot realize the forgiveness of God because they can find no forgiving spirit in those around them. It is useless to say that they ought to go straight to God. The truth is

they need the bridge of our forgiving friendship before they can cross the chasm that lies between them
and Him, and God needs that bridge that He may
make them conscious of His forgiving love. It is
not always easy. We sometimes tell ourselves we
must wait till they are penitent. But God did not
wait for that when He sent Jesus. Our Lord came
and died on the Cross, breathing forgiveness, in
order to awaken the penitent spirit. And it happened. For the dying thief heard the prayer and
saw on his face the love which pain and malice could
not kill. God became real to him there and then.
He saw that face as it had been the face of God.
"This is my commandment," said Jesus, "that ye
love one another, as I have loved you."

VII

AN ACT OF GOD

"He sent from above, he took me,
he drew me out of many waters."
Ps. 18: 16

THE laws of shipping have a strange way of describing a storm that wrecks a ship. They call it "an
act of God." It is their way of describing what is
outside of man's control. But it is a very limiting
thought of God. David the Psalmist had a wider
view. He saw in his victory over Saul, by which his
life was saved, an act of God. God had intervened
on his behalf. It may be asked by what right he or
any of us can claim to see the hand of God in our
lives. The answer is simple. How does a man know
that the series of notes that make up a Beethoven
Sonata are music? He has his own code, his own
trained musical sense. As Browning says, "The rest
may reason and welcome. 'Tis we musicians know."
In the same way, the man who lives in communion
with God has a way of interpreting life that is unknown to others. He has an inner sense by which he
reads in the events of life the signals of God's care
and love. So David interpreted this event. It was
God who did it. It was an experience as real as

41

when a hand is stretched from a river bank to pluck a drowning man from the floods. "He sent from above, he took me, he drew me out of many waters."

The Bible is one long story of the activity of God. It is not man who is the hero. It is God. God is always at work for people who trust Him. He is always intervening, doing things for them, working miracles of deliverance. We have largely lost this note in our thought of God. To us He often seems to stand back from life. He is a kind of encouraging spectator. It cheers us to think of Him there, looking on and wanting us to win. But He does not seem to act, and we have lost the habit of expecting Him to act. But the Bible gives us a different picture. It is more like Browning's picture of Him:

> God the strong, God the beneficent,
> God ever mindful in all strife and strait,
> Who for our own good makes the need extreme,
> Till at the last He puts forth might and saves.

We get this thought of God also in the story of people who have taken risks for God. The lives of great missionaries are full of it. In the Life of Hudson Taylor, for instance, we are not reading about what he did, but what God did. He saw a vision of God's plan for China which needed twenty missionaries and the money to send them out. He set out to find them in the spirit of consecration, and a banking account was mysteriously opened in London for his mission. It was an act of God. Two years

42

ago, three women missionaries set out across the
Gobi Desert in obedience to Divine guiding. They
had hairbreadth escapes. Their days were filled with
emergencies. But always "Something Happened,"
and that is the title of their book. It is the story of
the acts of God.

There is something here worth thinking out. Our
Western virtues are the active virtues. We urge one
another to get things done. We are always restless
to do something. We are very busy creating machinery and spending time and strength in keeping
it going. But somehow we often get the hollow
feeling that there is much bustle and noise without
any real things happening. A good deal of our
Christian service is like that, and we are often discouraged and wearied and ineffective. We forget
that all the real achievements in the Kingdom of God
are acts of God. This does not mean that we need
not work, or that we have merely to sit with folded
hands waiting for God to work. On the contrary,
God needs our service at its best. He wants one
hundred per cent efficiency. But that activity must
come from an inner dependence on Him, which keeps
our hearts at rest. A steam engine must be bolted
down to a bed of concrete before it is safe to set it
going. Without that basis of rest it would shake
itself to pieces in no time. So it is with us and God.
Dr. C. H. Dodd, writing about St. Paul's work and
experience, puts his finger on this point. "The im-

mense energy of the religious life is rooted in a moment of passivity in which God acts." The experience of salvation is always an act of deliverance. It is something which God does. This word of the Psalmist describes it: "He sent from above, he took me, he drew me out of many waters."

If we have no experience like this, there may be various reasons. We may not be expecting it. Our attention may be ourselves. We fight with doubt, for instance. We try to argue ourselves into belief, and it only increases our confusion. The way out is by opening our hearts and consciences to Christ in his life and his Cross. His coming was an act of God. And in Christ, God has still the power to reach us in the deeper levels of our spirit, and make us sure of Him.

It is the same with sin. For when we look deeply, the problem of doubt may lie there. The way into a real religion does not come by examining the way we think, but the way we live. And when we become conscious of sin, no fighting will help us. It is by coming to Him in our despair and putting ourselves into His hands, that we are set free. It is an act of deliverance. "He puts forth might and saves."

Another reason may be that we are not living on the level where emergencies can happen. We are too sheltered. We may not be attempting anything that needs the power of God. There may be no room in our little word of service for Him to act, for we can

44

do it all ourselves. The great men of faith were always in emergencies. They would have been utter failures apart from God. Their lives were full of miracles, because they were full of tasks that demanded it. Is not this where our poverty of experience lies? Hudson Taylor had one principle which directed his life. We are to seek the Kingdom of God, not the means of getting it. God will provide the means. He has promised that if our hearts are set on the Kingdom first, all the things we need shall come to us. When we take some road of service or obedience that "makes the need extreme, God at the last will put forth might and save."

VIII

THE PLACE OF RECOVERY

*"And Abraham went on his journey to
Bethel, unto the place of the altar,
which he had made there at the first."*
Gen. 13: 3, 4

One of the notable things about the Bible is its
honesty. It never conceals the faults of its heroes.
The incident of Abraham's fall in Egypt is not a
pleasant story. How could one who had given life
up to walk in God's guiding have fallen so l w that a
heathen king should rebuke him? Someone says
that every man has his strong point and his weak
point. It is helpful to remember this. We have
each our weak point, perhaps more than one. Therefore let us be charitable toward others and watchful
with ourselves. For our temptation is to be harsh
in our judgment of the weaknesses of others, and
merciful toward our own. We may even use the
weak points of others as a screen to hide from us
the truth about ourselves.

But the point to notice is the way in which Abraham recovered from his fall. He did not grovel in
self-contempt, or cover himself with reproaches.
Still less did he fall into that despair of himself which

is often only the outcome of wounded pride. He had given his life to God at the beginning. The symbol of it was the setting up of an altar. And his way of recovery was to go back to the place of the first altar and begin again.

This renewal of dedication to God points to the way of recovery for us all. We all know something of the humbling experience of fall and failure. We began with an act of self-surrender to Christ. That is the real beginning of the Christian life. It may be very simple, but it marks the parting of the ways. All the best things—love and work and service— spring out of that surrender to Christ. But we go out from that altar expecting life to be completely new and completely victorious, and we find it is not so. There are places where we lapse. The old weakness trips us, or one which we did not know was there. What are we to do about it? There is only one place of recovery. It is the altar where we began at the first.

This need to go back and make a fresh surrender may be very disappointing. I have known people who were so discouraged that they felt like giving up. They had the feeling that their first dedication had been a useless thing. We have all to realize, as a great saint said, that "the perseverance of the saints consists in constant beginnings." But it may further help us to remember one or two things.

For one thing, that first dedication to Christ was

47

not merely an act of our own resolution. It was not just our own will making a vow. Something happened there from the side of Christ which made it a covenant between him and us. We gave and he received, and he never lets go. It is there we find our comfort. St. Paul found his peace in the assurance of that grasp of Christ. "I am persuaded that he is able to keep that which I have committed unto him." That was his security. And when he had failed, he began again. "I press on to lay hold of that for which I have been laid hold of by Christ." When we honestly gave ourselves, we were laid hold of by him. That is the one secret of assurance. We cannot find peace by resting in the completeness of our own surrender. That is just a form of the old false way of trusting in our own good works. Something was done, in the region of our contact with Christ when we gave ourselves to him, that can never be undone. It is as vital as the life that is born when the plant we put into the earth has found living contact with the soil that receives it.

> Let me no more my comfort draw
> From my frail hold of Thee,
> In this alone rejoice with awe—
> Thy mighty grasp of me.

The next thing to remember is that our surrender is never complete, for we do not know ourselves. We have handed over to Him the keys of the citadel, and he has occupied it. But there are places where the old enemy still holds out, and must be dislodged by degrees. There are weeds in the garden that must still be uprooted, even after we have given it up to Him. There are rooms that must still be opened to his entry, which we did not know that we were keeping locked. We find out these things in the experience of life. From one point of view, growth in the Christian life is a gradual discovery of ourselves and our weaknesses. As we meet life with Him, our fears, our pride, the lurking places of self-will, are shown up. It is good to know ourselves and be honest about it, whatever it may cost in humiliation. For only so can we find points of contact with His grace. We have this for our comfort, that "where sin abounds, grace doth much more abound." There is nothing in us we need fear to face, for there is nothing from which Christ cannot deliver, if in sincerity we bring it to his love and are ready to have him take it away.

But above all, when we go back, let us remember the love to which we return. The way forward is to look from ourselves and from our shame to Him. It is to look at his love till it finds power to penetrate the secret places, the underground cellars, where, like a fungus, pride and fear are living. Only thus can we really make a surrender. For only love can win our wills. Only His self-giving to us on the Cross can enable us to give ourselves fully and deeply to him.

49

The true place of the altar of recovery and release is the place called Calvary. "This hast Thou done for me." That is the irresistible appeal. Dan Crawford tells of an old friend he met in Africa, "a fragile-looking figure with a Pauline gleam in his eye. 'I came to pay my debt,' he said. And there you have the secret in two words." The Cross had broken through to his heart, and set him free in a surrender that was joy. The altar where we can give ourselves fully is the altar where He has first given Himself to win us and set us free.

IX

SEEING AND BELIEVING

*"Blessed are they that have not
seen, and yet have believed."*
John 20: 29

THERE is a familiar saying that "seeing is believing."
That is what Thomas, the doubting disciple, said
when they told him that Christ had come back. He
said that he would not be convinced unless he could
even put his finger into the prints of the nails. When
the time came, however, and this proof was offered,
he refused to do it. The love and patience of Christ
with him broke down his resistance. He cried out
in adoring faith, "My Lord and my God." Jesus
was very understanding with Thomas. He knew
how difficult faith often is. He accepted this slow-
grown faith. "Because thou hast seen me, thou hast
believed."

But Jesus also said that it is possible to believe
without seeing. He called this faith a blessed thing.
"Blessed are they who have not seen, and yet have
believed." It is a great comfort to know this. For
all belief, since his appearances to his first disciples,
is of this kind. The world which crucified Christ
never saw him again. The crucifixion was a tragic

success from their point of view. Only to a few friends did he return. But others who did not see him came to believe. Since then, millions have believed in him though they have not seen. They have spoken of him as "whom having not seen, we love, in whom, though now we see him not, yet believing, we rejoice with joy unspeakable and full of glory."

How can we believe without seeing? We often feel that faith would be so easy if we could only see Christ. If only he would meet us on the road as he met the two disciples, how radiant our faith would be! If only he would come in visible form to us when we gather in church! It would be so easy to face temptation and sorrow if we could get a glimpse of him. Faith seems so needlessly difficult.

There are many things, however, that we believe in though we do not see them. We believe in truth though we cannot see it. We believe in love though we cannot see it. The realities of the spirit are things we cannot see with the outer eye. We do not even see beauty with the physical eye. We see the daffodil or the primrose. But it takes more than the outer eye to see their beauty. It needs what Wordsworth calls the "inner eye." Those whose inner eye is blind or unopened cannot see beauty. He describes such a man:

A primrose by a river's brim
A yellow primrose was to him
And it was nothing more.

There are people who are blind to love and goodness in others. One whose life is full of love may
live beside them for years and they may never see the
love. It is the lack of the inner eye. Many people
did not see the real spirit of Christ when he lived on
earth. They saw his form on the street. They heard
him speak. But to them he was only a man, a
peasant, perhaps a troublesome disturber of the peace.
He was nothing more. The inner eye was blind.
They saw, but did not believe.

Perhaps we reply that those who see beauty see
also the form which reveals it—the daffodil or the
primrose. They who see love see also the person who
is so full of it. That is our trouble. If only we
could see the form of Christ and get a glimpse of
him in his physical presence. But he does not appear.
He is hidden from us beyond the centuries.

> We long for the touch of a vanished hand,
> And the sound of a voice that is still.

But He is not so hidden as we imagine. His physical
form is gone. But its place is taken by the Gospel
story. There we see him in action. We listen to his
words. We watch him as he goes to Calvary. We
have only to open our New Testament and we are in
touch with him. His grace still comes to us through
these pages. A picture of paint and canvas can bring
beauty to our souls as truly as the actual woodland
scene which it represents. It is the same beauty

though the medium is different. So it is with the Gospels and the physical form of Christ. The medium is different, but the love is the same. His living Spirit uses the Gospels to speak to us. There we hear again the Voice that is still.

Again, Christ meets us in people who are like him. St. Paul saw Jesus reflected in the dying face of Stephen. He felt Christ's love in Stephen's prayer for the forgiveness of his enemies. Through these, Christ was in touch with him. We also can find touch with him through the fellowship of those who love him. That was his promise. St. Paul called the Church the "body of Christ." It was something more than a picture or a phrase. It was the description of a fact. For his Spirit dwells in the fellowship of his followers. Many have met him there. Like Thomas, they have found him where his disciples are gathered together. There, as one said, they have felt a Power at work "in which the evil in me was conquered and the good raised up." In the Sacrament also he comes. In that communion, his hand is stretched out to give us the bread which is the token of his sacrifice. Pierced for us, it comes through the shadows to offer this gift. It is from him we take it. In that gift we know the touch of his vanished hand.

Of course, belief needs something more. It needs our trust to make it a reality. We must not only see the love, but rest on it, and walk in the light of

54

it. That is essential. It is this that makes faith difficult. For we are often unwilling to step out in this trust. It is often hard to hold the light steady. It often means a fight to hold it, but it is "a good fight," as St. Paul said. By that light held steady we see our way. By this faith in Him we overcome the world. This is part of its blessedness.

Here and now faith is its own reward. But beyond the earth, when the physical is gone, the inner eye of faith will be the light of all our day. We are in this world, in point of fact, to develop and train this inner eye. We are here for this one purpose, to use and deepen our capacity to see the Unseen and Eternal. Unless that is happening, however brilliant may be the lights of earth, we walk in darkness. The reward of this exercise of faith will appear when the lights of earth have gone out forever. "We shall see him as he is, and when we shall see him we shall be like him." That is the final blessedness of those who see not and yet believe.

X

THE OPENING OF THE EYES

*"One thing I know, that, where-
as I was blind, now I see."*
JOHN 9: 25

ONE of Christ's most frequent miracles was the
opening of blind eyes. St. John gives a great deal of
prominence to one such case. Sight is so great a
blessing that we can understand the thrill of its recovery. To be able to see the world after years of
darkness was for this blind man a miracle. He could
see the world as it is, the faces of friends. He could
find his way along the roads. Everything became
new. It had all been there before. The difference
was that his eyes had been opened to it.

But St. John's emphasis on the physical miracle
had another reason. It was Christ's characteristic
work to open the blind eyes of the soul. To have
our eyes opened is a familiar experience. We can
all remember a time when in reading a story by
Stevenson or Scott our eyes were opened to the world
of romance and imagination. The dull facts of history or geography became the gateways to a hidden
world. Or we may remember a day when our eyes
were opened to the beauty of nature. We took a

walk with a friend who loved nature, and as he spoke of the sunset or pointed out the beauty of a flower, the glory of it all flashed into our mind. Our eyes were opened. There was a time also perhaps when the darker side of life was unveiled before us. We read a book about the slums. We listened to a talk by one whose heart was full of love and pity for those victims of our city life. For the first time we saw, behind the grimy dwellings, the struggles and tragedies hidden away in crowded cellars or back-courts. Our eyes were opened.

But the worst form of blindness is that which keeps us unaware of the realities of the spirit—goodness and truth and love. The trouble is that we may be blind and not know it. Mr. H. G. Wells has a story about a land where everyone was blind. But they did not know their defect. It is a picture of the condition in which many people live, in part at least. That is the reason why men and women do such dreadful things to one another. Hate blinds them for the moment and they kill. Passion blinds them and they dishonor themselves and others. When the passion fades, they see what they have done and are ashamed. Or, it may be, someone with the spirit of Christ comes near them and their eyes are opened to the poor, mean, squalid lives they are living. That was what happened in Palestine when Christ went among people. Their eyes were opened and they saw what goodness was and also what sin was. Some

57

hated their sin and turned to him. Some refused to face the light, and hated him and went back into the darkness. That is his power still. He can open our eyes if we will let him. He can show up the real world—for he alone of all men could see the world and God as they really are. He came into the world to open our eyes to what is really there.

When that happens what do we see? Many things become clear. For one thing we see ourselves as we are. It is not easy to know ourselves. We have often a false idea of what at heart we really are. Many people carry in their minds a picture of themselves which is not true. They may get it from the esteem of other people which they have accepted without question. They may have succeeded in life and been favored with various gifts. They come to imagine it is all due to their own good qualities. They live in the light of this false picture all their days. It makes them critical of other people and charitable to themselves. Most of us are self-deceived in this way. But if we really looked within, we might see something very different. We might see vanity and selfishness and worldly ambition. Christ opens our eyes to ourselves if we are willing. For when we come into his light and see ourselves in it, the mask drops off. Our secret desires become revealed. We see our love of comfort or self-pleasing. We see how eager we are for praise or flattery. It is not a pleasant thing to face. But it

58

is the only way to health and to reality. If he is to make anything of us, he must begin with us just where we are.

But when Christ opens our eyes, we see other things. We see the beauty of the life he can lead us into. We see what we might be to others. Best of all, we see him. It must have been a thrilling experience for the blind man to see the real world for the first time. There would be some unpleasant discoveries. Some things would be so ugly that they would almost make him shut his eyes again. But the most thrilling discovery would be to see Jesus who had opened his eyes. Have we really seen Jesus? Some people have not. They have some idea of him in their minds. His form stooping over a crippled man, his broken body hanging on the Cross. But the picture may have no reality. It does not live. His power to save, his unchanging friendship, his invincible love—that is the reality. But they have not really seen him. His face is like the image on a photographic plate, printed there in early years, but never developed. We may need to go into the dark, like the plate, before the image will shine out. We may need to pass through the black hour of self-knowledge. There are other experiences, too, like the acid touch of sorrow, which may help to make him real to us. But his Holy Spirit can make that hidden image clear. He is at work in all our hearts if we will let him. There is a prayer that can bring the awakening to his love and power. "Lord, open our eyes, that we may see." If we pray that prayer in sincerity, thinking of Him, the scales will fall. We shall see him by our side waiting to lead us into the real world with him.

XI

HOW CHRIST COMES TO STAY

*"They constrained him,
saying, Abide with us."*
Luke 24: 29

Two of Christ's disciples were going back home
after the crucifixion. They had pinned all their
hopes on Christ. They hoped that he was going to
do much for the world. "We trusted that it had
been he who would have redeemed Israel." So they
told one another. Now, that dream was over. But
just then a Stranger joined them and invited their
confidence. Something about him made it easy for
them to tell their trouble. They unburdened themselves to him. They confessed their broken hearts,
their faded hope, their tortured faith. As he talked
to them their faith came back; their hope revived and
their hearts were comforted. It is always so when
we begin to get near to Christ. The very roots of
life are renewed. The frozen springs begin to flow
again as when the summer sun breaks through the
wintry skies. Then they reached their dwelling and
invited the Stranger to come and spend the night
with them. "They constrained him, saying, Abide
with us." When the meal was set on the table he

took the bread and broke it. In that action they recognized something familiar and they knew they had made a guest of Christ.

It is a lovely story. But it suggests a question. Can this happen to ourselves, and how? What will it mean in our experience? How can we constrain Christ to come and dwell with us? Most of us know something of the influence of Christ. There are moments when he makes our hearts burn within us. There are times when we also are kindled by his courage and touched into unselfishness by the thought of his love. But these moments pass. The emotions he awakens are often very fleeting. We get back to the rush and tumble of life and they fade. We go back to the office or the workshop and his presence is forgotten. The old habits, fears, irritations get hold of us again. Christ does not become an abiding Power. He is not a steady, continuous influence in our life. How can he come to stay?

We must, of course, ask him to come in. He promised us the gift of his Spirit for the asking. We often forget that fact. We need not be content with what we are. He will come to dwell within us. A man was talking to a friend of his about his life. He had been making great unhappiness for himself and others. When he was shown a better way he said, "But that means that I must become a different kind of man." "That," said his friend, "is precisely what Christ came to do for you, to give you a new spirit, his own." Have we ever definitely invited Christ in? Have we asked him for his own spirit?

But if we are to ask Him in we must take some definite steps in the matter. We must, for one thing, take means whereby he will influence our thinking. We cannot expect Christ to become a living Power in our life if we are content to keep our old ideas. What about our outlook on life, for example? A good deal of trouble may lie there. There is a Christian view of life, of money, of suffering, of the whole purpose of life. Christ has a different view of these things from that of the world. We must take steps to get that outlook. If we only think of life as an opportunity for enjoying ourselves, or finding pleasure, or making money, no amount of praying will give us power to face it with faith and courage. We must bring our ideas to the light of his teaching. We must learn to think as he thought about people and the world and God. Have we the mind of Christ? It is part of the work of the New Testament to help us think like him. He has not got very deeply into our life till he has changed the currents of our thought.

We must also let Him into another part of the house of our life which we may be keeping closed to him. Every house has a basement or lumber-room where we store the things we do not want to have lying about the home. The house of the soul has also its basement. There we keep secrets the world does not know. It may be some hidden **fear** or grudge. It may be some buried sorrow that we have never really faced and overcome. There it **lies** in the basement, poisoning our soul with bitterness or unhappiness. Some unconquered passion **may be** there also. It may be kept under lock and key, **but it** is still there, never really overcome. We are ashamed of it. We try to forget it. But it is there. Some times it breaks out and makes trouble in our life. We must let Christ into that hidden part of life. Opening it up to him will be in itself a relief. But facing it with him will show us how to deal with it. If something there is wrong he will help us to put it away. If it is unhealthy, he will cleanse it of the poison. He may even turn it into a friend.

But yet, again, we must be prepared to accept His friends. We must make room for other people. He will want to widen our sympathies. He will ask us to make room in our hearts for all sorts of people whom we have been keeping outside. That is one of the things that happen when Christ comes in. We begin to think of people and care for people who were strangers to us before. When Kagawa, the Japanese Christian leader, asked Christ into his life some very strange guests came with him. He began to have a burning compassion for people in the slums of Kobe. He took a room among them. He took in criminals and drunkards. The house of his heart was enlarged.

It may be that the first step to invite Christ really

in is to take a living interest in other people. That was his own suggestion. "I was a stranger, and ye took me in." So he tells us he will say to some people at the judgment. And when they would ask him in surprise, "Lord, when saw we thee a stranger, and took thee in?" he would reply, "Inasmuch as ye did it unto one of the least of these my brethren, ye did it unto me." It may be in that disguise he is standing at our door waiting for us to invite him into our heart. But the point is that when we open the door in any of these ways he himself comes in. He has many ways of knocking. We may not always recognize his hand upon the door but behind these appeals to think, to be honest with ourselves, and to be kind to others, he is standing with his lamp and his love. He is a Guest who always gives more than he asks.

XII

WHEN THE FLOODS COME

"He that heareth these sayings of mine, and doeth them, is like a wise man that built his house upon a rock: and the floods came, and it fell not."
MATT. 7: 24, 25

THE question is sometimes asked whether religion makes any real difference to life. Some of us could answer that question for ourselves with gratitude. But it is pointed out that there are many whose lives are kind and decent, but who have no interest in religion. There does not seem to be much difference between these and many others who are devoutly religious. Much could be said on this point. It could be shown, for instance, that many people are living by ideals which religion has created and kept alive.

But one clear answer appears in this familiar picture of the two houses. Externally they were both alike. They both appeared to be strong, well built. and comfortable. The difference was in their foundations. One was built on sand, the other on rock. And this became clear when the floods came. For when these dark waters swirled round the foundations, the house built on sand tottered and fell. But

66

the floods beat on the house that was built on rock and it stood the strain.

The message of this picture is that faith gives life stability. It puts us in possession of secret resources. It enables us to stand up to the big strains of life. The weather of life will not always be so good as we imagine in our dreams. There will be storm and tempest and flood. It is then that the foundations of life will be tested. And only faith and the life which is built on it will enable us to stand the strain.

There are various kinds of stability which faith gives to life. One of these is moral stability. The real foundation of moral strength is faith in God. Our final support in the face of some gust of passion or the appeal of evil is the knowledge that the moral law is the command of God. All sin is against Him and His will of love for us. We are sometimes startled by some big moral lapse on the part of one whose life had seemed to be on a high level. How could it happen? If we knew all, we might find that there had been some loosening of the tie which bound him to God. He had given up prayer. He had ceased to bring his life into the light of God. Or perhaps there never had been any religion at the roots of his life. For the strength of religion is not merely the support of a theory. It is the security of an experience. Knowing God in Christ and following His guiding brings into life a joy and a peace which hold the heart against the appeal of evil. It ceases

67

to have any attraction for us. We have seen through it and know how shoddy it is. It can find no foothold in the heart which is held by the love of Christ. Temptation sometimes comes like a flood, rising in a moment and threatening to sweep us off our feet. But if we know Christ we have in us a power which will hold us secure.

Faith also gives us stability in the face of life and its troubles. There are various ways in which people react to the serious strains of life—a great sorrow or a big loss in business. Some people go to pieces. The very foundations give way. They lose heart and hope. They fall into self-pity or resentment. Despair takes hold of them. And in that hour they may betake themselves to self-indulgence. Moral disaster can sometimes be traced to some misfortune which we had no power to meet and which loosened the bonds of self-restraint.

Others meet misfortune with a kind of cold courage or obstinacy. They just grin and bear it, as the saying is. But the joy of life is gone and they become hard and sometimes bitter.

There is a better way. It is the victory which faith gives. The real joy of life is not touched. We know that God is with us, and with Him we are able to meet the worst with calmness and hope. We know that somehow He can enable us to find good in the evil, and through the burden to find a blessing. The character which faith creates is like good steel. The more it passes through the fire the harder it becomes, the more finely tempered it is for the service it can do. The house built on the rock of faith stands firm and solid, and in its shadow others whom life has broken find refuge.

But there is stability also in the face of death. We do not like to think much about death, but it is the one inevitable thing. And it is the most devastating of all the events that befall us on the earth. "Thou carriest them away as with a flood." So wrote the Psalmist. Only one thing can outface death—the faith in God which utterly rests on His love and care. Only the character which is built on His grace can endure amid the dissolving flood. Lockhart's description of his conversation with Sir Walter Scott when the latter was dying is almost too well known to quote. But it is worth recalling. "Read me something," said Scott. "What shall I read?" "Need you ask? There is only one book." Only one book, and his library at Abbotsford stacked from floor to ceiling! There comes a time when there is only one book. And then Scott added, "Be a good man, be religious; nothing else will give you comfort when you come to lie here." Only one place of comfort, one place of security, when the flood comes down the valley!

Some may say that it is morbid to live with the possible troubles and sorrows of life in view. But facts are facts. And the fact is that this is a fleeting

69

world and these changes belong to its nature. They are the symptoms of its transiency. "Here we have no abiding city." There is just one thing to do. As a great scholar says, "We are forced to become natives of the Kingdom of Heaven." That is life's clearest message and that is its deepest meaning.

XIII

CROWDED OUT

*"There was no room
for them in the inn."*
LUKE 2: 7

IT is one of the most poignant facts in history that
Christ was born in a cattle shed. When Mary and
Joseph came to Bethlehem, tired and weary, there
was no room for them in the inn. Mary needed,
at that moment, all the care that human tenderness
could give. But no one offered to give up his place
for the stranger. When the infant Christ sought
entry to the world for which he died, he was crowded
out.

Time and again that incident would come back to
Mary's mind. It became a portent. It was a sign of
what was to come. For when Jesus went out from
Nazareth to proclaim his message, the same thing
happened again. He was crowded out. There was
no room for him in the minds and hearts of men.
His truth could find no foothold in minds that were
crammed with prejudices and fixed ideas. There
was no room in their hearts for his leadership and
his love.

There are various answers to the question why religion has not a deeper hold on us today. If we were to ask a man who was indifferent to religion why he did not believe, he might say that he found faith impossible. He might even fall back on the old excuse of the faults and failures of religious people. He might tell you of a pious man who had done him down in business. He might explain that he had had too much of religion in his boyhood. But if he were quite honest, he would probably admit that he had not given the question any real thought. If we pressed him further as to the reason, the truth might come out. It is just that among the throng of other interests and duties, religion has been crowded out. God is outside his life because there is no room for Him within. That is the biggest handicap with which religion in our time has to deal. The minds and hearts of many people are preoccupied, and God is crowded out.

Think, for instance, of the hectic interests of the modern world. In the country, years ago, there were plenty of empty spaces, quiet spots of green. Now those places are being occupied with a variety of buildings. It is like that with the mind. A generation ago life had many quiet places. There was less to occupy the hours of leisure. Sunday was a close time for worship. But today, a dozen things clamor for our spare moments. There are new books to be read, new films to see, a stream of exciting entertainments to be enjoyed. These may not be unhealthy.

72

But they drain the mind of its energy. With the best will in the world, a mind that is occupied with these every evening has little taste for the things of the spirit, and little energy to give to prayer and worship. Some people cannot even get through a book that calls for any thought. Constant absorption in one line of things unfits the mind for other interests. Darwin said in his later years that his mind was "a withered leaf to everything except science." He could not even listen with enjoyment to the *Messiah*, which once had been able to thrill him. So it is with many people. The story of Christ has no interest for them. Its music strikes no answering chord within. The voice of God is crowded out.

There are some also who have no room for religion because of the pressure of life. When Moses came back to his people with God's call to an adventure of faith, they had no ears for him. "They hearkened not because of their bitter burdens." They could think of nothing except the struggle of life. The same is true today for multitudes. Making ends meet on a pittance involves so much worry and strain that the appeal of Christ can find no place. It may be business is going badly. Every day there is some new trouble to meet. The mind becomes absorbed with the problem of living. Or it may be that we are ambitious to make a career. We are full of plans for the future. We become immersed in the thought of success, or the comfort and position which it brings. If we have any need of religion, it does not make itself felt. Later, perhaps, we may feel it, but at the moment life is too full for any deeper voices to be heard. God is crowded out.

It may be, however, that we are aware of this need, and we mean to face it. We know that times of quiet are essential for us. We can no more get the best from life without giving time to God, than a traveler can get through the desert without oases of wells and trees, where he can rest his body and refill his waterskins. But somehow we never seem to get time. We are so busy with one thing and another. Most of them are trivial things that clutter up our life like papers on a desk. It is not that we want to keep God out or that prayer is uncongenial. It is just that we do not manage our time. Things drift over our life like sand blown across a garden, while we stand helplessly by. We omit the daily prayer. The New Testament lies in a corner, unopened for weeks together. We begin to slip out of the habit of Sunday worship. Bit by bit God fades out of our life, and the vital experience that once glowed in our hearts dies like a neglected fire. God has not been rejected; He has just been elbowed out by the multitude of other things.

Ten minutes of quietness and prayer every day would bring a revival of religion. The things that have power over us are the things to which we give our attention. This is as true of religion as of anything else. Christ will take his own place within us if we give him room to enter. There is no heart he cannot capture if he gets his opportunity. For there is a secret place which is all his own and which only he can fill. The idols of pleasure or fashion or sport that we put in his place will not fill that place. For a while we may not be conscious of it. But sooner or later the inner void will make its echoes heard. At the door of every heart that has not let him in, he stands with his lamp of love and joy. If we listen, we will hear his knocking. If we go on listening and thinking of him, we will become aware of his love and of our need of him. If we still continue to give him our thought, his love and grace will become irresistible, and then we shall open and let him in.

XIV

UNLIKELY OPPORTUNITIES

*"In such an hour as ye think
not the Son of man cometh."*
MATT. 24: 44

THERE are different views of the meanings of these
words of Christ. But we can find in them a message
for us all. He does come to us and to our world time
and again. He comes to our help, in some clear word
of guilding or in some flash of conviction that makes
us strong. He comes in the call to some way of
service and adventure. He comes in the crisis of decision, bidding us take his way. But however he may
come, it is a spiritual opportunity. It is a chance to
advance the Kingdom of God, or to rise to some
higher level of life in his fellowship.

"There is a tide in the affairs of men." There
are also tides in the life of the spirit. There are
moments of crisis through which Christ comes more
fully to his throne in the world and in our lives. The
point is that these moments often come when we do
not expect them. "God comes without bell," says an
old writer. "In such an hour as ye think not."

There is hope for us in this fact that He comes at
unlikely moments. We should never be depressed

76

by the look of things. The New Testament view of life is that our extremity is God's opportunity. The point of weakness may be the place of strength. For God's power becomes active when we are no longer striving to fight our own battles or have our own way. He becomes our Saviour when we have discovered that we cannot save ourselves. We are very slow to realize this. But if we look back we will find it so. The most unlikely situations have often been big with blessing. Nothing seemed to the Psalmist so unlike the hour of God's mercy as sickness and calamity. Yet when sore trouble had come and gone, he knew that God had been there. "It was good for me that I had been afflicted." We have all had this kind of experience. Sorrow blinded us and looked like crushing our faith. But somehow it opened up for us the reality of the eternal world. It brought God wonderfully near. Or we met with a difficulty that seemed insuperable. A blank wall faced us; but to our surprise we found a door opening that could only be opened by the hand of God. In such an hour as ye think not—in the dull, disappointing, disastrous hours—God comes.

This can be seen on a big scale in the great religious revivals. Things were dark enough in Europe when the dawn of the new day broke in Luther's soul. It was a most unpromising hour when the spirit came on John Wesley, and he went forth on his journeys. His diary describes things that were in the region of miracle. The most hopeless-looking places became seed plots of the Gospel. The most unlikely people were changed. This is surely an encouragement to hope. No hour is too desperate for God to make of it His opportunity. No night is so dark that His dawn cannot break. We live in the era of our Lord. So the calendar reminds us. The resurrection is not exhausted. His Spirit, planted in the earth through his life and death in it, has the power of endless revival, till the kingdoms of the world become his Kingdom. The more hopeless seems the opposition, the more hopeful it may be, for antagonism to Christ is often an inverted testimony to his power. "In such an hour as ye think not the Son of man cometh."

But this word is also a warning. Spiritual opportunities are often unexpected. They give no sign. We have to be on the outlook for them. Too often we only see them when they have passed. Perhaps we met someone who needed our comfort or sympathy. They were hungry for some word that would have touched their deeper need. But we did not notice. We were thinking of other things. The bitterest regrets that can visit us come from the realizing that we have failed someone in his spiritual need. It might be we lack the sensitiveness that comes through being "at leisure from ourselves." Christ had that sensitiveness in perfection. He read men's secret longings like an open book. His ear was always open for the undertone of heart-hunger that often sounds behind flippant words. He was always spiritually alert.

A business man writing about business says that "all progress comes by the new idea. But the new idea does not come with brass bands and banners down the street. It may be as silent and unobtrusive as the acorn-shoot breaking through the ground. We have to be on the outlook for it." Are we always ready to welcome the new idea, the truth we need, if it come in a shape we do not like? It is a curious thing that spiritual revivals are often started by unlikely people. When D. L. Moody went to Europe many people scouted the idea that God could use a man like him to reach the heart of England. He was an American, a layman, very blunt, without a college education. The newspapers of London were hostile to begin with. "Could any good thing come out of Chicago?" Yet within a few weeks the heart of London was vibrating with the Gospel he proclaimed. Are we willing to take Christ's challenge from anyone? Are we ready to obey his call though it come at inconvenient moments, in such an hour as we think not?

Christ was unrecognized as Messiah by his own people because he came in an unexpected way. The real reason was that they were not on the watch for God. Would we recognize Christ today? Are we sure that he is not coming to us, and that we are not missing his call? For his call to us will often come in ways we do not like.   And we have a strange way of being blind to things we do not like.   His way of love will be opposed to many of our prejudices.   His call for adventure in obedience will upset our conventional ways.   His message may be very inconvenient.   There are all kinds of reasons why we may be blind to him and not know it.   There is all the more reason to pray that when he comes, he will find us ready.

XV

A GOSPEL OF OUR OWN

*"Jesus Christ raised from the
dead according to my gospel."*
2 Tim. 2: 8

St. Paul was very fond of speaking of the gospel
as "my gospel." The phrase strikes a little strangely
on the ear. It sounds as if there are many versions
of the gospel, and every man might have his own.
When we come to think of it, we realize that it must
be so. The gospel in all its fullness is one definite
message. It is the old, old story of God's seeking,
redeeming love for men. But no two men will preach
the message in exactly the same way. Each will see
that love from his own angle. He will paint the
picture of it in the colors of his own experience.
God's love does different things for each of us. To
one it comes as the message that brings victory over
pain. To another it comes as the power that sets
us free from hate, or from fear, or from some habit
whose clutch is like the grip of miry clay. To one, it
is Christ crucified that takes the soul with wonder.
To another, it is the assurance of Christ risen and
living still. In that sense, each one will be able to
say "my gospel."

In point of fact, the gospel has not won us at all until we can say "my gospel." The Psalmist speaks of God as his own. He calls Him "my God." We do not possess the gospel till we have appropriated it. We do not know it till it has come as a message to our particular and burning need. A good many people can say what the gospel is, but it rings no peal in the belfry of the heart. "Right well hast thou described the composition of this coin," says one in Dante's poem, "but tell me, hast thou got it in thy purse?" That is the crucial question. God's love has no reality for us until at some point it has kindled the heart to music. It is not ours till it has met our need. As Francis Thompson says, there is no way "to pack and label souls for God." His grace in Christ must become an individual experience. Then only it comes alive.

The danger with some people is that they stop short of that point. Their gospel is their father's or their mother's gospel. The message is precious because it glows in the light of some dear face. Their religion is only lit by some tender and sacred associations. That is how it begins in the child's mind. God is mediated by the influence of parents or some revered teacher. But if he has never got beyond these to God Himself, God is only a second-hand experience. This religion cannot hold him in the big storms of life. It cannot enable him to stand up to the strain. It never sets him free to walk in a light that is his own. A gospel that we only revere because it has changed the lives of others will never bring real peace or power to ourselves. It must become our own, because at some point it has met us with saving power.

And, further, we cannot preach a gospel that is not our own. It will not get home to any soul in need. Is not this the explanation of much ineffective preaching? One man has all the equipment of a scholar. He knows theology through and through. He can set forth the message of the gospel with clear and accurate detail. There may even be eloquence in his words. But nothing happens. The hearers are edified and impressed, but that is all. Another speaks with halting words. His statement of truth is very incomplete. He has very little to say that would satisfy a theologian. But there is a thrill in his voice and a light in his eye that gets through to our souls. He has had an experience that gives wings to his faltering words and makes us forget his disjointed phrases. We know that the gospel he preaches is his gospel. This is the best test of our possession of the gospel. Is there that in it which we want to pass on? Have we something to say to people in need? Is there something that we can tell them of the grace of God, not out of a book, but out of our own experience? If there is not this power to say quite simply what Christ means to us, it may be well to ask ourselves if he means anything very deeply. More than anything, we need today a host of ordinary people who are able to say "my gospel." It has been said that every Christian life, in itself, is a fresh translation of the gospel. St. Paul told his converts that they were his "epistles known and read of all men." That is true, but it is not enough. What has the gospel done for us? Where has it met our need? That is what we ought to know. Then only do we possess a gospel. Then only have we a message for the need of men.

But we must be careful not to confine the gospel to what we know of it ourselves. That is the mistake some people make. They think their gospel is all of it. The gospel which St. Paul claimed as his was a very rich thing. We can see that if we take any page in his letters or look up the places where he speaks of his gospel. "O the depth of the riches of the knowledge of God," he says in one place. His passion was to know more and more of "the love that passeth knowledge," and "to be filled with all the fullness of God." We may not be able to put our gospel into the terms which others use. But may there not be something in their way of putting it which covers an experience we might also have, and which is waiting for us? Most of us are only saved in patches. Some have found victory over sin, but no victory over sorrow. Some have found deliverance from fear, but none from lurking pride. Some know the release from clinging guilt, but none from the censorious spirit. It takes a full gospel to meet the whole range of our need. A Paganini can make wonderful music from a violin with only one string. But even a genius needs four strings to make the finest music. The saints of the New Testament sang of One who had "loosed them from their sins and made them kings and priests to God." They sang of One who could "keep them from falling, and present them faultless before his presence." It was a full salvation they claimed and found. Have we claimed from God all He is waiting to give? The gospel which Christ brought means nothing less.

XVI

THE ISSUES OF LIFE

*"Out of the heart
are the issues of life."*
Prov. 4: 23

THE end of the year is a time when we look back,
and forward. How has it fared with us in the year
that is past? What have we gained or lost? Has
there been progress, or just stagnation? And what
of the future? What will the new year bring?
There is a veil upon it that we would sometimes like
to pierce, for us and for those we love. But God
has mercifully hidden the future from our eyes.
There is a way, however, in which we can make sure
that the past will bear its harvest of good, whatever
its events have been. There is a way, also, in which
we can make sure of the future. "Out of the heart,"
says the old preacher, "are the issues of life." In
other words, what is within will out.

This saying raises a question. What are the real
issues of life? In other words, what is it that is
being decided? When two people go to law, an issue
is raised. Something is being decided. The same
thing is true of life. Many events befall us as we
take our way through life. We meet with difficulties,

86

opportunities, gladness, and sorrow. Through all these things, something is being decided. It may be through various crises, or it may be through the slow influences of circumstances, that the issue emerges. But something is being decided. What is the central issue of life?

To this issue we are often blind. We may imagine, for instance, that the issue of life is whether or not we are successful in business, or happy at home, or are reaching some position of comfort. When we have won any of these things, we are apt to think that the issue of life is successfully reached. On the other hand, we may imagine, if none of these things happen, that life has failed. We think of it as frustration. It has come to nothing. A look at Calvary should dispel that illusion. For Christ was poor. He was lonely. He had no home or position in the world. He died in the prime of manhood on a criminal's cross. That outcome to his life should shake us free from our illustrations. If only we took him seriously, it would make us revise all our false ideas about the real issue of life. For in our hearts we know that his life was, of all that have ever been lived, the most completely successful. He had the gift of perfect peace in his own Spirit. He had the joy of complete fellowship with God. He had the most complete and balanced character. His personality was fully victorious over circumstances. When we think of him, we know that the real issue

87

of life is what we call character. It is the develop-
ment of our personality, the fulfillment of our true
nature into that likeness to him of which God made
us capable. The issue of life is character. What is
life making of us? What are we becoming under
the smile of good fortune or the blows of circum-
stance? That is what is being decided. That is
the central issue of life.

In the long run, character decides everything that
matters. It decides, to a large extent, what we call
material success. It decides the kind of influence we
have. If we think of the people who have won the
hearts and the loyalty of others, we know that the
secret is in what they were. For some of them were
poor. Many of them had little reputation. Some
of them had found little but disappointment in their
ambitions. But that indefinable something we call
character shone out. It brought them the trust and
respect of their fellows. And therefore it gave them
influence. For influence works through the channels
of trust and admiration.

Character also decides destiny. We cannot draw
aside the veil that overhangs the beyond. But we
have a key. Death will change many things. But it
will not change character. That persists. Jesus
made that clear. It was that fact which brought a
sob into his voice when he saw what the result of
some kinds of conduct were bound to be. But his

kind of character will last. It has survival value. Death cannot touch its beauty.

> Only the true and righteous soul,
>   Like seasoned timber, never gives.
> But when the whole world turns to coal,
>   Then chiefly lives.

But what is it that decides character? It is what lies within. It is the thoughts and motives and desires we cherish in our hearts. Within us all lie forces that decide everything. What we are within decides how we react to a situation. It decides whether we shall fall under a temptation or overcome it. It decides how we shall meet trouble or prosperity. We are not alive enough to the deadly nature of some of the feelings we carry within us. We take it lightly that there is jealously or pride or selfishness in our hearts. We do not see how deadly is their power to bring disaster on ourselves and others. Not long ago, the newspapers told of some children who had been playing with a live shell. They thought it was harmless, and for a long time nothing happened. But one day something must have touched the detonator on the sensitive point. The shell exploded, bringing destruction. That is what happens time and again with ourselves, and those forces that we permit to remain within. Temper explodes, and the happiness of home is wrecked. Selfishness breaks out, and we take a wrong road. Feelings of dislike and prejudice are touched by some incident, and a war ensues. What lies in the future? Let us look within ourselves and we shall know.

There is a gladsome message for us all about the secret rooms of our hearts. They can be swept clean of the evil things that bring disaster. What is in will out. But what is in us can be changed. Christ can dwell in the heart, expelling and controlling. That is the secret of hope, for us and for the world.

How can we help to direct the future for ourselves and others, so that it will bring nothing but good? Let us look within with the light of Christ to help us. Let us get rid of the debris of old enmities and resentments. "Search me, O God, and know my heart, and see if there be any wicked way in me, and lead me in the way everlasting."

XVII

FINDING THE CHRISTIAN WAY

*"And he said to them, Follow
me. . . . And they followed him."*
MATT. 4: 19, 20

WHAT does it mean to follow Christ today? That is
a question that is often asked. Many years ago a
book was written to try to give an answer to this
question. Its title was *What Would Jesus Do?*
Some critics replied that this is not the right question.
We cannot find out the Christian way for us by trying to discover what Christ would do. For he had
his own life to live in his own circumstances, and
we have ours. The question for us is rather, "What
would Jesus have us do?" But that is just as hard
to answer. Many people are seeking for explicit
guidance on conduct. So a B.C.D. interviewer told
some Christian leaders the other day. But can we
have such guidance from other people in everything?
Is there anyone competent to tell another exactly, in
all circumstances, what is the Christian way for him?

In the days when Christ was on earth it was simple
for his disciples. As they walked together through
the land, they listened to his teaching. They felt
the influence of his Spirit. They got to know what

he would have them do. If they were in doubt they would ask him. It was simple and easy then. But now,

> Dim tracts of time divide
> These golden days from me.
> Thy voice comes strange o'er years of change.
> How can I follow Thee?

One thing is clear. Christ was not a dictator. He did not make rules even for his disciples. He gave them principles. But they had to find out for themselves how these should be applied. He did not always answer their questions in so many words. He did not lead people as a blind man is led, step by step, by the pull of someone's hand. He opened their eyes that they might see for themselves. For, as someone says, "God's sheep are men"—not sheep. Time and again when he was questioned, he would throw the question back and ask, "What do you think yourselves?"

Are we then left alone? Is there nothing in our day that corresponds with the experience of His first disciples? The truth is very clear and very startling. We are in the same position as these disciples were. We have the presence and power of the Holy Spirit and the Holy Spirit, as St. Paul tells us, is the Spirit of Christ. The resurrection of Christ means for us his personal presence and activity in our hearts. For lack of grasping this truth of the reality and power of the Holy Spirit, we stumble and grope in the darkness. Christ even said, "It is expedient for you that I go away, for the Holy Spirit will come to you." We can be as near Christ today as were his own followers. We can have all they had of the reality of his Spirit.

But the Spirit uses means for our guiding. We must know the Bible, and especially the New Testament. The Gospels give us the teaching of Christ. They give us his principles. They bring us in touch with his own life. We can see him at work. We can watch him as he went among people. We can feel the throb of his heart. We come in touch with his mind. Through these pages, the very atmosphere of his presence invades our lives, as if he came into the room. We cannot have the guiding of the Spirit except through this knowledge of his mind. Some of the worst mistakes and blunders have been made because this was neglected.

The Holy Spirit also uses the Church—the fellowship of his followers. Individual judgment may be at fault. We may not see clearly. But through the fellowship of those who believe, we can be helped to find the way. It is in this quality of fellowship that the Church is often weak. It is true that light will often come in the atmosphere of worship. The eternal world breaks in upon us there, and we see things under its light. The Word of God can be heard in that hour when the voices of earth are hushed, and the fear and selfishness which blind us are banished. But there ought to be some group of people within every Church to which we can take our difficulty and ask their help. That is what Christ counsels. If we have a dispute with another and we cannot get the offending brother to see his fault, we should bring the matter before the Church. Why should not one who finds it difficult to know the will of Christ in business or home bring his problem to the fellowship? Without this fellowship the Spirit cannot fully guide us.

But in the last resort, guiding comes through our own mind and conscience. We must think out the matter in the presence of Christ. We must seek his will in prayer. We must have quietness enough to listen to his voice within. That quietness means more than just being still. It means being absolutely honest and utterly willing to do what he would have us do. He cannot speak clearly till the voices of self-will are silenced. Reason must have its place, but reason alone cannot guide us. For reason can be the servant of our own desires. We can find reasons for nearly anything we want to do. God wants us to use our reason. But, if it is to help us, it must be freed from the shackles of fear and self-will.

If we would find the Christian way, the first essential is that we must be ready to take it. We must be ready to walk in the light, or the light will not come. But "unto the upright there ariseth light in the darkness." If we are willing to do His will, we

shall know. The disciples left all and followed him.
For them, to follow Christ meant leaving home and
friends and business. For us, it means leaving our
own plans, our own wishes, our own fears and ambitions, and going out unfettered, with Christ. Then
we shall not be left in any doubt. We may make mistakes. But through these we shall learn. For we are
only learners at the best. To be a disciple just means
that.

XVIII

HIS LOVE AND OURS

*"This is my commandment, That ye
love one another, as I have loved you."*
JOHN 15: 12

IT is not Christ's habit in his teaching to define his
terms. He does not tell us in so many words what he
means by God. He does something much better.
He reveals God. In his own life and deeds he shows
us God in action. He did not come to add to our
knowledge about God. He came to enable us to
know God.

It is the same with His great word "love." He
does not define love and tell us in so many words
what it means. That is what we have to think out
for ourselves. It is very much needed today. The
word "love" has been so misused by sentimental
people, and by some who make it an excuse for passion and self-indulgence, that it has lost the beauty
and power which Christ gave to it. But he does not
define love. He does something better. He reveals
it in his own life and actions. As we look at him,
we see love unfolding into beauty like a bud into
flower. His one command was that we should love.

But when we ask what that means, there is only one answer: "Love one another, as I have loved you."

This ought to set us thinking. It ought to make us compare His love and ours. None of us is so poor as not to know something of the spirit of love. We fall in love and get married. We develop affection for one another in the intimacy of home or friendship. But our love is often a very imperfect thing. It is often mixed with elements of selfishness, though we may not be conscious of it. A good many troubles and frictions arise from this fact. The more love draws us to one another, the more we need to make sure that it is the real thing. Otherwise, the very nearness to each other into which it brings us will create strain and unhappiness. How does our love look in the light of his?

For one thing, His love was never possessive. He asked nothing for himself from those he loved. He was not seeking any subtle satisfactions of his own. But our love is not seldom mingled with selfishness. We seek to be loved. We look for affection in return for our own. We claim from our children respect or gratitude. We become resentful of things that seem to draw away their minds or affections from ourselves. We become jealous of friendships they may form which we cannot share. If we do this, we make a claim to which we have no right. Love asks no reward except the privilege of loving.

97

It will only fully come back to us when it seeks no return. That is the strange paradox of love.

Again, His love was never dominating. He did not seek to force his own ideas or plans on his disciples. He did not try to rule their lives by dictation. He knew that no obedience is worth while that does not spring from the love of what is right. But we often seek to dominate. We have our own ideas of what our children ought to be. We feel that we know what our friends ought to do. And we use all our power to shape them to that pattern. Such was not his way. "Not slaves, but friends," was his word for them. He forced open no doors. They opened to him from within, through the love that won its way into the heart and moved the will to make him Lord.

His love also was never soft. He did not try to save his friends from trouble or pain. "Behold, I send you forth as sheep in the midst of wolves." He knew it was good for them to face life and meet it for themselves. He knew the bracing power of the east wind of hardship. He knew that we only develop as we are forced to stand up to life. The best experience is something we must all buy for ourselves and pay the price. But our love is sometimes coddling. We would like to shield our children, to make life easy for them. We let them lean on us, instead of making them stand alone. That kind of love is a perilous gift. The birds are better parents than some of us. "The eagle stirreth up her nest. She scattereth her young." It is a painful process for them both. But it is the way to life.

Yet again, His love was never easy going. He always kept his friends up to their best. He would not make excuses for them that took the sting from conscience. He warned Peter of the weak spot in his heart, though it must have hurt him to the quick to chill that enthusiastic spirit. But our love is sometimes morally slack. We make excuses for those we love. We let them down gently. We tell ourselves that love is blind to faults. It is not true. Love is terribly clear-sighted. It sees so clearly things that are wrong that the burden and the sorrow of it fall on the heart like the shadow of the Cross.

And His love never failed. No matter what people were like or how they had wronged him or themselves, his love never failed. And this steadfast, unconquerable love for people was the secret of his power. In spite of all that others may be or do, we must never cease to value their spirit and to seek their good. It is this, more than anything else, to which he calls us.

How can we reach a love like His? There is only one way. It is to keep ourselves in the place where his love can reach us. When Stephen the martyr was dying, he broke out in a prayer that brings Calvary back to mind. His soul flamed into the very spirit of Christ. How did he reach it? The

99

secret was that he was thinking of Christ. He looked up to heaven, and there he saw Christ at the right hand of God. He saw him there, with the print of the nails on his hands and the thorn-scars on his brow. From that vision, a love like his was born. "So we," with all our selfishness and failure, "beholding the glory of the Lord, are changed into his image."

XIX

THE SECRET OF OBEDIENCE

*"If a man love me, he
will keep my words."*
JOHN 14: 23

THIS is a simple statement of fact. If we love anyone truly, we strive to do what they ask of us. It
ceases to be a duty and becomes a delight. Though
it may not be easy, it is no burden but a privilege.
Where the heart leads, the feet will follow. That is
plain fact. Love for people may lead us to do some
very foolish things. But that only reveals the power
which love has over us, and how it can capture and
hold us. Our will moves in the pathway of our
deepest affections. It was on simple love of himself
that Christ depended for the carrying out of his will
in the world, and on nothing else. "If a man love
me, he will keep my words."

The State has its laws, and for obedience to these
it depends in the last resort on force. It attaches
penalties to all its enactments. The reason is not
vindictiveness. It is not seeking merely to punish
a man who breaks these laws. It is seeking to
create the driving power by which men may be compelled to obey. It enlists the motive of fear. In

the last resort, it will step in to prevent the evildoer from further breaking of the law, by shutting him up for a while.

Christ used no such motive. Obedience compelled by fear or force would have been useless to him. For one thing, his commandments are not such as fear can enforce. He bids us love our enemies. No force can compel that miraculous spirit. Neither force nor fear can produce the compassion of the good Samaritan. Only love can do that. For another thing, the obedience that is not from the heart has no value for him. It means that the man within has never been won. It is only a "dull, mechanic exercise." The elder brother in the parable was of this type. His obedience was mere duty. His heart was not in it. Love had never been kindled. He was only a son in name. But where love is awakened, there is no doubt of the obedience. It is a startling thing that Christ relied on no other power than this for getting his will done. We often wish he had. When we look at the world around us, we cannot understand how God can let its wickedness go on. It is a common problem. Sometimes it comes home with tragic bitterness to ourselves. We see a friend we dearly love becoming the prey of evil passions. We feel so helpless. And what is more, we have the feeling that God is helpless also. Doubts of his power begin to gather. But there is one unfailing spring of moral power. "If a man love me," said Christ, "he will keep my words."

That is true of every man. It does not matter how twisted the nature or weak the will. As a matter of fact, the power of the will is only the power of the things that are allowed to capture our hearts. But in Christ the supreme source of power is open That is why he came. God offers us in him a spring of power that is unfailing.

> For Oh! my Master is so fair,
> His smile so sweet to banished men,
> That they who meet Him unaware
> Can never turn to earth again.

That love is open to all. There is no one to whose nature Christ cannot make appeal, if the chance to know him be given. We should have no gospel if this were not true. He has always and forever the power to awaken in our hearts the love of himself. Phillips Brooks tells in his letters of a visit he paid in early life to Dresden, to see Raphael's "Madonna." He had been thrilled by it. Years later he returned, wondering with some fear if the first impression would be repeated, and the same thrill capture him again. He was afraid lest the threat and strain of the years should have dulled his feeling for its beauty. But to his joy his early experience was renewed. There is that in the beauty of artistic genius which has eternal appeal. The same is true of Christ in the spiritual world. He has eternal appeal. Can

any human heart pass so far into the shadows of
moral death that it will be forever cold to him? He
did not believe it. Somehow, if only he gets his
chance, the flame will kindle. And when love to him
kindles, there will be no trouble about keeping his
commandments.

It may be there is a message here for ourselves.
The power to live in Christ's way is in the depth and
quality of our love to him. That love has nothing
sentimental about it. It is adoration, worship, reverence for truth and goodness. But there is in it
also devotion to himself. That has always been the
secret of the power of Christianity. It is more than
loyalty to principles; it is devotion to a Person.
Where our life has been deficient in moral power, it
has been because the spring of love within the heart
has not been touched. It may be that we have been
breaking down at some point or points. Somehow
we have found ourselves lacking in moral power.
Or it may be that we have tried to follow and to
keep Christ's word, but the way has been dull and
hard. The glow has gone from our hearts, or else
it has never been there. "If a man love me," said
Christ, "he will keep my words."

It may be that is what is lacking. We need to let
Him kindle the flame or renew it. That is his power.
There is no other way of coming by this experience.
"We love him," said Paul, "because he first loved
us." That is why he came and lived and died. His

104

love was the fire God cast on the earth to set our hearts aflame. "God so loved the world, that he gave his only begotten Son." That is the very core of the Christian religion. His purpose was that "whosoever believeth on him might have everlasting life." The closer we come to Christ in prayer, worship, and obedience, the more our love to him awakens. And that is the source of everlasting life.

XX

GOD'S TOOLS OR HIS PARTNERS?

*"I girded thee, though
thou hast not known me."*
Isa. 45:5

THIS was God's word about Cyrus, king of Persia,
by the lips of Isaiah the prophet. He had just done
a remarkable thing. When he captured Babylon, he
found the Jewish exiles there, and set them free to
return to Jerusalem and rebuild it. He was the
means of their deliverance. No doubt he had ends
of his own to serve. He did not in the least understand that in this action he was the instrument of
God's purpose for Israel and the world. Serving
his own designs, he was really fulfilling God's plan.
"I girded thee, though thou hast not known me."

This trivial act of his was the one thing that gave
his life distinction. We do not always know the
deeds in our life that are really important. We may
build a big business, write books, and do other things
that loom large in the public eye. But the things
that really count in our life may be some little un-
considered acts which we did by the way.

> Just this or that fine impulse,
> Which for once had play unstifled,

Seems the sole work of a lifetime,
That away the rest have trifled.

Some eloquent obituary notices will not count for much in the light of eternity. But the obscure deeds of some unknown people will stand out because they have been links in the chain of God's purpose. Those who did them may be unconscious that they were doing anything splendid. Christ's words on the final judgment come to mind. "When saw we thee hungry, and gave thee meat? or naked, and clothed thee?" So these anonymous servants of his will ask. And his reply will be, "Inasmuch as ye did it unto one of the least of these, ye did it unto me."

The only thing worth living for is to be used of God. The keynote of our prayer should be that He may use us. Some of us need to learn this lesson. We are so apt to think of prayer as a means of bringing God to our aid. When we pray, we may really be trying to make use of God. We set up our little plans for happiness or success, and ask that God should aid them. That may be to make religion the ally of selfishness. Prayer has far larger objects in view. God is calling us to come forth out of the stuffy room of our own little plans into the wide world of His purpose. True prayer asks to be used of God for what He wants done.

This opens up a very important question. Are we to be God's tools or His partners? Dr. John Oman in a sermon says this startling thing: "All alike are

107

God's instruments. By no desire of evil or doing wickedness with both hands can we prevent God from using us." There is a sense in which we are all God's instruments, His tools. He makes even the wrath of man to praise Him. He uses our selfish plans, and schemes, and ambitions to work His will. Jeremiah pictures Him as a potter who makes bowls and cups on his wheel. The clay may prove refractory, and the thing he is making may break in his hands. But the potter is not beaten. He takes the clay that has refused to be molded to his first design and makes of it another vessel, "as seems good to him to make it." God is like that potter.

It is a very encouraging truth. Even those who seem to be working against the Kingdom can be used of God. We should remember this when our hearts fail us for fear that chaos is in control.

But He does not want to use us merely as tools. For tools are blind, unconscious things. They have no idea for what they are intended. And when they are done with, they are cast aside. God wants us to be His partners. He wants us to co-operate with Him, to understand His will, and to use all our minds and our strength in working along with Him. The real question of life is not whether God will use us. It is in what way we shall be used. Shall we be His tools or His partners? That is the choice of life.

The difference between the two is very simple. A violin in the hands of a player is a tool. It does not know what he is doing with it. It cannot feel the music that he is producing as he draws his bow across the strings. But that player in an orchestra is a partner. He enters into the mind of the conductor. He catches his spirit. He is alive with the music they are making together. He has ceased to be a tool and become a partner.

The choice meets us day by day in life. It meets us in our daily work. We can be merely tools there. We can be just a hand in a factory, a bit of office furniture. We can go through the day driven by the whip of necessity. Or we can see God's purpose to use our labor to get things made and done for His children. We can make work a partnership with God.

It is the same with other things. Our life can be the plaything of various currents and desires. Sympathy can move us to kind actions. Circumstances can drive us to this course or to that. We can be the slaves of fear, or pride, or ambition. God will use us there. Some fine things have been done with very poor motives. But He has a great purpose in the world, and He wants us to share it. That is the message of Christ. He came to call us into a life-partnership with God.

A century ago a great Scottish scholar was much troubled about whether Christ was really sent of God. One day brooding over the question, it suddenly flashed upon him, "God means us to know His mind." That is why He sent Jesus. God means us to know His mind for the world and for ourselves. He is eager to guide us, to whisper to us His plans for every day. Shall we give ourselves to be partners with Him?

XXI

GOD AND OUR PAIN

*"The cup which my Father hath
given me, shall I not drink it?"*
JOHN 18: 11

MANY of the sayings of Christ are windows into his
own soul. We are grateful for them all. But for
none are we more grateful than for those in which
we discover how he faced his pain. For, sooner or
later, in some form, we must meet pain too. No one
has been through the mill of experience in which
souls are made till he has suffered. If we can meet
it as he met it, we can ask nothing more; for then we
can be sure it will not be wasted.

There are various ways of meeting pain. One is
the stoical way. It is just to shut our teeth and bear
it with a hard kind of courage. One of the best
examples of this way in modern times is that of the
poet Henley. When he was a young man, one of his
feet had to be amputated and the other was threatened. For nearly two years he lay in Edinburgh In-
firmary while Lister, the great surgeon, employed all
his skill to save it. In the end he succeeded. But the
process was long and painful in the extreme. Con-
fined to his bed during these long months, Henley

111

spent his time writing poetry. One of these poems is
very familiar. He calls it Invictus—unconquered.

> Out of the night that covers me,
>> Black as the pit from pole to pole,
> I thank whatever gods there be
>> For my unconquerable soul.

So it begins. The courage of it fills us with admiration. He defies pain to break his spirit. There
is something very noble in this kind of courage. But
when we turn from this attitude to that of Christ,
we feel a difference. His spirit was something more
than unconquered, it was victorious. There was a
serenity in him, a peace, which we miss in the other.
Furthermore, in Christ's spirit there was no defiance
of pain. There was something far better. There
was a willing acceptance. He took it into his heart
and made something beautiful out of the experience.
He tells us his secret. God was his Father, whose
love was the greatest thing in his life. From his
hands he took the pain that came to him. "The cup
which my Father hath given me, shall I not drink it?"

There is something in this description of His pain
that challenges us to think. For this is the last way
in which we would describe what he passed through.
The cup had been mixed by other hands than God's.
Men who hated him had prepared it for him. More
than physical suffering was in it. Scorn, hatred,
malice—all these were in that cup. How could he
say it was the cup which his Father had given him?

112

We can see that he met with suffering because he took the way of love. He encountered it on the way of duty. In that sense God gave it to him. God took it, as it were, filled with the agony that men had put into it, and put it into Christ's hands.

So also we can accept our pain from the hands of God. It makes a world of difference to be able to take it from His hands. There is victory in that way of facing suffering. To do this is more than to be unconquered by it. It is to find the secret of overcoming it.

There is no other way of finding peace in the heart of pain. Our chief need is to learn how to face it, not to explain it. When we attempt to find an explanation for suffering, we often try to keep God out of it. We say that it is not His will that calamity and misfortune should darken the earth. The other day the world was startled by an explosion in a school in Texas whereby four hundred children were killed. We say that God had nothing to do with it. That horrible destruction of human life was certainly not of His deliberate doing. Some human carelessness or neglect must have been the real cause of it. That sounds reasonable. But can we say that God has nothing to do with it, that He is out of it all? The message of Christ to these bereaved parents would certainly be clear. "It is not the will of your Father that one of these little ones should perish." But would he say nothing more? Surely he would say this: "Not a sparrow falleth to the ground without your Father." That carries us a step farther. God's love is at the foundation of the world. All that is in it came out of His heart and purpose of love. He put us into the world knowing the tragic possibilities. But His love also has power to take these things and use them for our good. Behind all He rules, and His love has a purpose that can only be achieved through suffering. Whatever happens, we must not surrender our belief in the sovereignty of God. Whatever happens to us, no pain that we suffer comes to us except through those Almighty hands that mix it with blessing. If we but have the faith to take it so, there is a sense in which we can only find peace by taking it from Him and saying, "Thy will be done."

It is a great mystery. But light breaks through if we can see the love behind. Even now we can find some value in pain. Are there not qualities produced by it that can come in no other way? We have all met with people who have not suffered deeply in their own lives. The world has gone smoothly for them. But the result is a kind of hardness and shallowness in their spirit as if the depths had never been broken up. One feels that they have missed a vital experience. There is something specially tender in a mother's affection for her ailing child that is not found in her love for those who are healthy and strong. Without that pain he would never have known the infinite wonder of her love. Pain has the power to enrich and deepen our very joy. In a novel, Mr. Aldous Huxley describes a world from which suffering has been excluded by science. The hard edges of life are smoothed by drugs. No one suffers. It is a dreadful picture of a shallow, sordid earth. There can be no such thing as "Christianity without tears." There is a note in Miss Adelaide Proctor's lines to which our hearts respond. We know them to be true.

> I thank Thee, Lord, that all our joy
>   Is touched with pain;
> That shadows fall on brightest hours,
>   That thorns remain;
> So that earth's bliss may be our guide,
>   And not our chain.

The present experience may seem to be "not joyous, but grievous: nevertheless afterward it yieldeth the peaceful fruit of righteousness." That is the gift which God's hand puts into the cup of pain. But there is this also, without it we could not know the depth and glory of His love.

115

XXII

FIRST THINGS FIRST

"Seek ye first the kingdom of God; and all these things shall be added unto you."
MATT. 6: 33

CHRIST puts his finger here on the real trouble of the world. It is that we are not putting first things first. There are some commercial products that are only found when men are seeking something else. They are called by-products, and they are sometimes the most valuable products of the factory.

It is the same with many of the things which we seek in our own lives. Happiness, for instance, is a by-product. That is a fact which is often forgotten. A good many people seek happiness by pursuing pleasure or ambition. They gather possessions round them. They spend time in devising means of enjoyment. But they fail to find happiness. It eludes them all the time. One day, however, they forget themselves and their happiness, and seek to help other people. Or, perhaps, they lose themselves in a bit of work they are doing. Then, all unawares, happiness steals into their hearts. Happiness is a by-product. It is found by seeking something higher than itself. Forgetting it and ourselves, we find it.

116

The root of a good deal of futile strain and disappointment lies here. We are not putting first things first. Life is like a tangled bit of string. It only unravels itself when we take it up by the right end. All round him, as he talked, Christ saw men with the strain of life on their faces, and anxiety looking out of their eyes. They were victims of the struggle of life. They were afraid of tomorrow. They were haunted by the thought of poverty. The more they strained, the more entangled they became in worry and anxiety. They were taking life up by the strong end. "Seek the kingdom of God," said Jesus. Put first in your life the desire to be ruled and guided by him, and what you vainly seek by selfish struggle will come in its own place. God will provide. That is the way the world was meant to work. We must put first things first, and the secondary things will follow in their place.

This is the clue to most of the problems of life. It is the secret of peace for instance. Peace cannot be found merely by seeking it. For peace is a fruit. It is a result. It comes when we seek first what God wants. It is the condition in which we find ourselves living, when together we seek God's way in our national ambitions. Mr. Aldous Huxley said this in a recent talk on the subject: "Peace is the by-product of a certain way of life." There is a life in fellowship with God which "takes away the occasion of all

117

wars." It cuts the roots of strife, because it sets us seeking things that cannot be secured by fighting.

It is the same with our material needs. Christ was a realist in the true sense of the word. He knew these needs that lie behind the struggle of life. He knew the sting of poverty, and the anxiety of the breadwinner thinking of his children. He himself had carried on the business for his widowed mother for some years. He did not suggest that man should lie back and dream and expect God to provide. But he saw deeper than all of us. He saw that the cruel poverty of many people is largely the result of the selfish struggle that makes men seek so feverishly for money and things. The result is to produce a hold-up of business in which many suffer poverty. What is needed is to ease the strain. That of itself would make the machine move smoothly and freely for all. Fear is a useful safeguard against danger. It is a cruel tyrant when we make it the motive of life. It paralyzes our powers. It makes us hard and cruel to others. God would set us free from it by leading us to trust Him with our cares, and to give ourselves to do His will. He bids us put first things first. And the first thing is to seek His kingdom, not our own satisfaction. If only we took His way, we should find power and wisdom to solve all our problems of poverty. The machinery of supply would move freely, because it would be working in God's way

We can try this principle out in our individual lives. People smile at old-fashioned ideas of Providence. But very few have tried them out. Those who have really put God first and left the rest to Him know that he cares. Perhaps we have some perplexing thing to face A task lies ahead of which we are afraid. The more we think of it the less we feel able to face it. But suppose that we took Christ's way and just sought to follow his will. A sense of peace would come into our hearts that would give us both quietness and power. We would find also that the mountain that looked so great became a molehill that we hardly noticed at all. Or suppose we took this way in the troubles that come in our relationships with others. There are misunderstandings that inevitably arise between us. There are frictions that come when we work together. There is only one way out. It is to put God's kingdom first, and not our own plans or our own pride. The people of ancient Palestine thrashed their corn at a place on the high hillside. They chose it there that the wind might blow aside the chaff as they beat the corn, and leave the pure grain. If we kept our fellowship with others on the high plane of God's kingdom, the wind of His Spirit would blow away the chaff and dust of our frictions and misunderstandings.

This is not mere human strategy. God is at work. Seeking His Kingdom we are preparing His way.

119

We are making in the desert a highway for the Almighty love. We are opening our lives to the Divine Omnipotence. He is waiting to work in us, through us, and for us, if we will fulfill conditions. And the chief of these is that we put first things first.

XXIII

IF WE HAVE NO LOVE

*If I . . . have not
love, I am nothing."*
1 Cor. 13 : 2

THIS is a very startling statement. We all know that in the Christian character love is the essential thing. That would be accepted by everyone. The man in the street knows that. The highest praise he can give to anyone is to call him a real Christian. He may have a very vague idea of what he means. But when you examine what evokes this praise, you will find that it is always some act of love. In this chapter St. Paul is drawing a pen picture of the spirit of Christ. Every line of that picture is some aspect of love. There is no doubt that love is the central quality of the Christian spirit. If we have no love, we are not Christian. We may be good or kind or brave or wise, but we are not Christlike. We are of those who in the last day will hear him say, "I never knew you."

Do we really love people? It is a searching and salutary question. Do we really care about people? Some of us care about truth. Some care about right. Some care very much about peace. But do we care about people? Have we a deep and vital interest in others such as gives them a real place in our lives? Do we really value people as individuals? There is something very challenging about this question. It goes to the roots.

If we want a method of testing this, we can do it by turning St. Paul's description of love into a series of questions. Are we easily provoked? Are we puffed up? Do we suffer long and are we always kind? Do we seek our own? Do we ever rejoice in iniquity—some unholy gossip about others? Above all, does our love ever fail? Are there people whom we just give up and put out of our life? These questions test the reality of our love.

It is good to face them. For without love we have no real power of influencing people. We may, of course, get them to do what we want. We may force our own views on them if we are strong enough. But without love we cannot help them deeply. The problem that faces every man who would help people is how to bring them to God. That is the service that gets to the heart of every need. We may be eloquent, but that will not be enough. St. Paul found that. He knew the futility of mere words. As Bacon puts it: "Talk is but a tinkling cymbal when there is no love." We may be very efficient in church work or social service. We may be able to run clubs, or teach a class, or organize a meeting with great success. But if we have no love, nothing real gets through.

The heart is not reached.   God is not revealed.   For God is love and only love can reveal Him.   Only love can mediate His spirit.   No amount of energy will light a candle if there be no flame.   And love is like a flame.   Sometimes that love has to blaze in self-sacrifice before it can set the hearts of others alight with the glory of God.   Christ knew that.   It was the reason why he went to Calvary.   For there his love found a flashpoint where it was strong enough to melt the hardness of selfish hearts.   There it had power to burn through the blindness and bondage of sin.   Without that love, service remains feeble and ineffective.

But St. Paul goes further, and this is the startling thing.   He says that without love we are nothing.   This is very strong.   What does it mean?   It means that without love we have no personality.   We have no character.   We do not count.   We have never really developed.   The psychologist will support this view.   He will tell us that without love we are not really grown up.   We may be old in years.   But that has nothing to do with our true life.   Some people are childish at thirty.   They are still self-centered.   They want their own way in everything, and are upset if they do not get it.   They have not awakened to the value of others.   They may use others and depend on others.   But these others have no real value for them except to be used for their comfort or gain.   A child in its early years is the center of its world.

123

Others exist only to satisfy its needs. But as it develops it becomes aware of the rights of other people. It feels a duty toward them. It begins to care for them. That marks the stage of growing up. But until that happens, the child is undeveloped. Personality begins to awaken in response to the needs of other people. We can no more grow into it by any method of education or effort of ambition without love to others than a climbing plant can grow without something to climb on. We need people to whose service and interests we can give ourselves if we are to find life. We become ourselves as we give ourselves to others. For we were made for one another. We are not persons in the true sense of the word unless we are giving to others what they need from us, as well as receiving what we need from them. Without love we are nothing.

That is what this word means. We are told in another place that love is the bond of perfectness. Other qualities of character are important. But it is love that holds them together. Love is the keystone of character. It is like the stone at the center of the arch that holds the other stones in their place and keeps the arch strong and beautiful. Take it out and the arch will fall into a ruin. Love is like that. Without it we have no inner unity. The forces of life within us have nothing to bind them into one and make our character Christlike. Without love we are nothing.

To apply this standard to our life may be very humbling. It may bring us to despair. There is nothing so humbling as to discover how little we really care about people. And this is most deeply true when we think of our love in the light of Calvary. Yet it is good to apply this test. How do we stand in relation to those around us? What about our attitude to those in the home? We must not take for granted even our love for them. What about those who serve us? Or what of the people we try to help? Do we really care about them? It is very humbling to face this standard.

But we need not despair even if we find how selfish we are. For this love can be awakened. It can be kindled. That is the gospel. There is no other way, in fact, to get it. It is a gift which we can only get from Christ. If, having seen the self-love that holds us in bondage, we take our hearts to him, he will give us the power to love.

XXIV

TRUTH WILL OUT

*"There is nothing hid
that shall not be known."*
Matt. 10: 26

Nothing is surer than that truth will out. That is
one of life's most familiar facts. It was one of the
convictions on which Christ did his work. He used
it to comfort the disciples when he sent them out to
preach. He knew the reception they would meet
with. Their message would be scorned; they themselves persecuted. The world would have none of
them. But they must not lose heart. One day the
truth would win; for truth will out. "There is
nothing hid that shall not be known."

This is the faith in which all knowledge has been
sought and found. Research is going on in every
department of science. For years, experts have been
working to find the cause and cure of certain fatal
diseases. Up to the present they have been baffled,
but they keep at it. They are sure that some day the
truth will out. Nature has no secrets that will not
yield, in time, to the mind of man. Every year some
new truth is unfolded. So it will go on. There is
nothing hid that shall not one day be known.

This ought to give us fresh hope in the battle with every kind of evil. One day, the method of ending war and poverty will be discovered. Perhaps it is truer to say that the secret will be accepted by all. For the secret is already in our hands in the message and way of Christ. The trouble is that his way is hidden by our blindness and our unwillingness to follow him. But one day the truth will come home. Other ways than his will prove useless. There may be much suffering and disappointment to pass through before men are ready to see his way and to take it. But sooner or later the truth will out. This ought to give us hope and courage to go on in Christ's service. His secret will yet unfold itself as the word of life. The truth cannot be hid.

This fact has its message also about our inner life. What is within will come out. The secret things we carry in the heart will make their presence felt. We sometimes talk of the dead past. But the past is never really dead. It has its influence on the present. In one of the quadrangles in Oxford there is a sun-dial with this inscription in Latin: "Done, but not done with." That is true of the past. The things we have done and been are not finally buried. They go with us to comfort us farther along the road. Something happens to a child that gives a shock to the mind. Nature closes the wound. The child forgets all about it. But in later years, this unpleasant experience soaks up into the mind like damp into

127

the walls of a house, producing fears and shadows. We cannot finally conceal what is hidden in our hearts. A selfish spirit, a wrong motive, will stain through. Unwholesome thoughts will break into the light, however we may try to hide them. Some people have a weak spot in their character that has never been overcome. One day they meet a crisis, and the weakness shows up. They take the easy road. They fail their friends. They go down before temptation like a rotten tree in a gale. Ruskin tells of a sculptor in Venice who was engaged to carve statuary high up in a building. He had a dishonest streak in him, and left the hidden side of the statues unfinished. Apparently he "got away with it," as we say. The fraud was not discovered. But the dishonest streak was his undoing. Some years later he was banished for forgery. What is in will out.

Is not this the truth behind the doctrine of the Last Judgment? One day, "the books will be opened." What is hidden will come to light. What we really are at heart, so we shall appear before the judgment seat of Christ. There is only one way to meet this relentless fact. It is to open our hearts, here and now, to the light of truth. It is to be honest with ourselves, with conscience, with other people, with God. There is a way in which our hearts may be cleansed within. His light is the antiseptic for every evil motive and desire. "If we confess our sins,

128

he is faithful and just to forgive us our sins, and to cleanse us from all unrighteousness."

There is another side to this principle. It is just as true that a Christlike spirit will out. What is in us of his nature will come to the light. A really Christian character will have its influence. A loving heart cannot be hid. John summed up the victory of Christ in these words: "The light shineth in darkness; and the darkness could not smother it." When we think of it, it is sheer miracle that the influence of Christ has survived. He was a peasant from a village in Galilee. He had no standing in the world of his day. He was without money, or learning, or position. The big man in Palestine was Pilate, the Roman governor. He looked on Christ as a harmless man who had raised a storm in a teacup. Anatole France has an imaginative study in which he tells how in later years Pilate, retired to Italy, met an old friend. They talked of former days in Palestine. The name of Christ came up, but Pilate had completely forgotten the incident. He could not even recall Christ's name. Yet today, in a world full of resounding names, his is the Name that is above every name. Pilate is only remembered as the man who sent him to the Cross.

It may be that some of us are disheartened by the ineffectual fight of faith. What is the use of keeping our hearts from evil? Why go on making these unseen sacrifices that some of us make? Why keep on with prayer? Why trouble about this inner life of communion with God? The world cares little about what goes on in the secret places of our souls. But do not let us lose heart. The strongest power in the world is the life of God in the soul. All that is best in it comes from that hidden spring. The most effective thing we can do for the world is to tend the light in the heart, which through prayer and His word the Spirit of God keeps burning there. That light will one day conquer the darkness. It cannot be hid.

XXV

CARRYING OUR OWN PACK

"Every man shall bear his own burden."
GAL. 6: 5

THIS is a bit of sound common sense. The word "burden" originally meant the pack which every soldier must carry. He has no responsibility for leading the campaign, but at least he must carry his pack.

There is a burden of responsibility which belongs to each of us. It is good to be brought back to this fact. So many things are done for us in these days, there is danger that we expect to be carried, instead of walking on our own feet. Every child should be taught to do some things for himself. He should be made to carry his pack, however small it be. Among the Laplanders when they travel each one carries his own pack, which is proportioned to his strength. The training for this duty is begun in childhood. The tiniest child from the day he can walk has to carry his pack. And the size increases as he grows. It is a sound principle.

There is one burden in particular which cannot be evaded. We cannot escape responsibility for our own character. A good deal is known in these days about the forces that influence us. Some of these are inherited. There are qualities of disposition which come from our parents and grandparents. There are influences also that come from our surroundings. The friendships we form, the training we receive in home or school, all play their part in shaping our lives. Psychologists also tell us of unconscious forces that work in the mind, affecting our behavior and our moods. We should remember these things when we are judging others. It should make us very charitable and understanding. But we must not take shelter in these things from our responsibility for choosing the right path. In many cases where we have gone wrong, we know that it was we who chose that way. The odds against us may have been heavy. But it was we who finally made the decision.

We may not have much freedom, but we can at least put ourselves under the right influences. We have at least the freedom to bring ourselves under the power of Christ. "God hath provided a way of escape," says St. Paul. We can turn to Christ and give him the chance to become Master. We can seek the way out of our prison house which is offered us in prayer. Since Christ has come, no man need go on being bound by wrong habits. He has made it possible for us to be free if we will only realize his power. Many people are like a little dog I saw the other day. He had been tied up to a post by a leather leash, which, for want of something better to do, he had bitten through. But he sat quite still because he did not realize that he was free. There is freedom for us in Christ if we will take it, and for accepting it the responsibility is ours. God has put upon us that burden of choice.

> The sweet compulsion of His voice
> Respects the sanctity of will.
> He giveth day; thou hast thy choice
> To walk in darkness still.

Christ is very clear about our responsibility. Behind all his teaching and pleading there is the shadow of the Great White Throne. We shall be judged for what we have allowed life to make of us. His teaching about the Judgment is the message of our responsibility. It is also the assurance of our dignity. We are not just driftwood on the tide. We are the children of God. We have a real part to play in God's purpose. That burden is really a gift. It is our chance of winning true manhood.

But we have a pack to carry in our influence on the world. When we think about the world we live in, we may at first be paralyzed. We can see, of course, the possibility of influencing the little world around us. We do put something for good or evil into the spirit of the home or the workshop. We count as individuals there, and we are responsible for the influence we have. Many a man or woman has brought a new spirit into a home or an office which has changed the whole atmosphere. But when

133

we think of the great world beyond, we seem so helpless. How can we by speech or action change the currents of fear or hate that are so strong? It seems like trying to stem the flow of a great river by throwing stones into it.

But let us think a little deeper. The kind of world we live in is made by the kind of people who live in it. And everyone counts. We speak of fear or hate as if these were forces in themselves. But there is no such thing as fear or hate. There are only individuals who fear and hate. If people were changed, these forces would be gone. There is war in the world because we are afraid or are not at peace within. There are slums and poverty in the world because we are selfish. And every individual counts.

Perhaps we say that if everyone were like us the world would be different. But would it? Are we sure there is no hate in our hearts toward others? Have we no prejudices against people? Are we always unselfish in the little things that make up our daily life? We only need to bring our lives into the full light of Christ to see the roots of the sin of the world in ourselves. When Isaiah, the young aristocrat, had his eyes opened in the temple, he saw the sin of his nation. But first of all he saw his own. "Lo! I am a man of unclean lips, and I dwell among a people of unclean lips." He saw that if he were to help the world he must begin with himself. He must let God deal with him. Then he could play his part in changing the world. The springs of good and evil are within ourselves.

In a village where each house has a garden, every householder has his own plot to cultivate. If one neglects his garden, the weeds from it will infect the rest, blowing over with the wind. But those who make their gardens beautiful inspire the others to do the same, till in time the whole aspect of the place is changed. That is how a new spirit may come in a whole community or nation. God seeks to change the world by changing us one by one. For that change in ourselves we are responsible.

We may not think we have much influence. But God uses individuals. Great reformations have always come through individuals. There is no limit to what God can do through one life given up to Him. For it is God who works. It is through us He finds entrance to some part of His world. Before the door of our individual hearts He stands, seeking a way through us into the world beyond. That door we have to open to Him. Our responsibility for a new world lies there.

XXVI

THE VALLEY OF HUMILIATION

"He made himself of no reputation; he humbled himself, and became obedient unto death, even the death of the Cross."
PHIL. 2: 7, 8

WE are all agreed that the world would be a better place if there were more people in it like Christ. Life would be different in many respects for ourselves if we were more like him. But have we ever seriously thought what it means to be like Christ? Our picture of him is often very vague. He is so big, of course, that no one can really describe him. We cannot put into words what God put into a life. There is one aspect of Christ's character which we may forget. St. Paul captures and holds it before us in a few sentences. It is his humiliation. If we are to be like Christ, we must be like him in this. We must also take the way of humiliation. "Let this mind be in you, which was also in Christ Jesus, who made himself of no reputation, and humbled himself, and became obedient unto death."

Think of some points in this picture. "He made Himself of no reputation." He was willing, for love's sake, to lose caste, to let reputation go. There are all sorts of instances of this. He made friends with publicans and sinners. He won for himself the name of the sinners' friend. That title rings with music. But it cost him his reputation. The responsible people looked down on him for it. "Birds of a feather flock together." So they said of him. Or think of how he touched the leper in order to heal him, and how he spoke kindly to the woman with an issue of blood after she had touched him. We fail to realize the full import of these simple acts. But he incurred thereby the charge of ritual uncleanness, which in the eyes of the religious authorities was one of the worst of crimes. A scholar says that of all his miracles of love there were none greater than these.

Or think how he spoke quite frankly to his disciples of his temptations. He was ready to confess —and to them, his pupils—that he also knew the inner conflict with the spirit of evil. He acknowledged that he was subject to like passions with them. They had put him on a pedestal. But he would not stay there, if by coming down to their level he could help them to win their battle.

The crowning instance was that He humbled himself to take the way of the Cross. That was the supreme act of his passion to serve men. The Cross has become a different thing since Jesus died on it. It has become a symbol of glory. We fashion it in gold, and cover it with jewels. We print it on our banners and carry it in processions. We wear it as the proudest of our ornaments. But the cross in his day was the equivalent of the gallows in ours. No man could think with any satisfaction of going out of life that way. It would surround his memory with ugly and degrading associations. Only criminals were crucified, and with criminals he hung on Calvary. He was even deprived of the distinction that might have come from dying alone. He submitted to death, even the death of the Cross.

We have only to think a little to realize how far we are from being like him in his humiliation. How hard it is for us to take a stand that will make us lose caste with others, or to provoke their scorn. If we are to follow him, we will need to be willing to lose reputation. We must be willing "to go with him without the camp, bearing his reproach." Again, how hard it is for most of us to confess that we are wrong, or that we have been mean or ungenerous or spiteful. We do not like to give ourselves away. We imagine we may lose influence with people. We like to keep on our pedestal.

It is often in this humbling of our pride that the way of the Cross becomes most real. To bear the Cross means the death of self, and self is generally most deeply entrenched in the stronghold of pride. But it is here that we find the surest way into the kingdom of God. The passport of our own good deeds will not give us entrance there. In the light of Christ's face the best we can be or do looks cheap and poor. The gateway into the kingdom of grace is always open. But when our heads are high with pride or the sense of our own good deeds, we are not lowly enough to pass through that open door. It is when we discover that we have nothing of our own to bring except the cry for mercy and forgiveness, that the grace of Christ becomes the light of all our day. Only those who walk the way of humiliation can see the love that brings a smile of gladness to the face, and puts a song in the heart.

But only the way of humiliation can bring the spirit of fellowship. Only thus can we find the secret of reconciliation. There is a story in the life of Aggrey of Africa which illustrates this fact. This distinguished negro had borne many humiliations. He had had to submit to treatment by ignorant white people that brings a blush of shame to the cheek. He had borne it all with a smile. But his greatest hour of triumph was that of his own self-humbling. He had to address a band of college teachers who had fallen out among themselves, and was asked to say a word that would help. He told them of an experience of his own. On one occasion he had been rude to his wife in the presence of her sister. He felt, of course, that he must apologize. But it came to him that the apology must be made where the wrong had been done, in the presence of the sister who had been witness of the wrong; and this he did. It must have cost him a good deal to make this confession, and a good deal more to tell the story of it. But at the close of the address, there was a rush on the part of those of his listeners who had been estranged to make friends with one another. The way of humiliation is the road to the healing of bitterness. It is the way for the world. It is the way for us all. And if we find it hard to humble our pride, Christ has provided the power by which it can be done. "He humbled himself, and became obedient unto death, even the death of the cross." The picture that can melt our pride is there.

> When I survey the wondrous Cross,
> I pour contempt on all my pride.

XXVII

REFUSING EXEMPTION

*"Others were tortured,
not accepting deliverance."*
HEB. 11 : 35

THIS phrase opens a window upon incredible heroism. These Jews were fighting for their faith with a ruthless enemy. They suffered cruelties which the writer only hints at. It was one of the high moments in the story of faith. It adds to our admiration of them to know that at any moment they might have had release. They had only to give in, perhaps to make a little compromise. How tempting it must sometimes have been! Does God really mean people to suffer these tortures for the sake of a conviction? Is not one religion as good as another? One can imagine such thoughts, like bats in the twilight, darting about their minds. But they refused exemption from suffering at the price of surrender. They stood fast, not accepting deliverance.

We may think there is very little in their situation that is like our own. That may or may not be the case. History has a way of repeating itself. There are Christians at this moment in Europe and in Asia who are in exactly the same position as these tortured

Hebrews. One day it may be our turn to face the same conflict of loyalties. There are places in life even now where we must take the same stand, and refuse to accept deliverance. There are burdens from which we must refuse exemption. If life is to be fully lived, for instance, there are risks we must be ready to take. We cannot expect to be secure from all the ills of life. We shall have to face the possibility of illness or pain, or hardship or anxiety. Such things come inevitably through taking life with both hands, not shrinking from its call. Work brings its burdens. Family life has its own troubles. If we fling ourselves wholeheartedly into any worth-while task, it will take it out of us in labor and strain. There is no other way of becoming what God is seeking to make us, or of finding the deep secrets of a satisfying life. We can escape only at a cost. The cost is that we cease to live in any real sense. It is to be

> left in God's contempt apart,
> With ghastly smooth life, dead at heart,
> Tame in earth's paddock as her prize.

We may find it hard at times not to complain, if only to ourselves. But it will give us courage if we realize that some of our heaviest burdens are the price of fullness of life. "Count it all joy," the Apostle dares to say, "when ye fall into divers trials." With this in mind we can meet trouble cheerfully.

142

We can turn our backs on the easy road with a willing heart. We can refuse to accept deliverance.

Again, there is no exemption from trouble and burden if our hearts are to be active in sympathy. It is a strain on the spirit even to read the newspapers of a morning. If we use imagination at all, life will cut very deep into our happiness and peace of mind. Real sympathy costs. There is a constant temptation here also to seek exemption. We turn our minds away from things that shock us. We tell ourselves it is none of our business. Some of our amusements are mechanisms of escape from the pain which comes to sensitive minds. But that way lies the loss of one of life's best gifts—the power to love and help other people. A modern novelist tells the story of a young girl who found this out. She was herself loved, but had no love in her own heart. After marriage she found herself in a cholera-stricken district in China. The suffering around her took her heart and softened it to sympathy and care. Then she made the discovery that the greatest gift in life is not to be loved but to have love in one's own heart. If we are to know this power of loving, we must not seek exemption from the suffering of others. We must refuse to accept deliverance.

There is also the temptation to seek exemption from the troubles and burdens of faith. We cannot take it for granted that the days of persecution are over. What has been happening in other parts of the world has smashed that pleasant illusion. The day of bitter conflict may come for all who take Christ seriously. We may have to decide whether we are to be true to our faith and take what will come to us, or seek exemption through compromise.

But that temptation faces us now in other ways. It is not easy in these days to be an out-and-out Christian. If it is easy, we may wonder if there is not some lack of reality about our loyalty. The Christian way is not popular, for one thing. The habit of religion has gone out of fashion. Definite work for the Church means the sacrifice of time and energy for something which many people round us will probably regard as matter for jest. The Christian way does demand some austerity with ourselves. There are some tempting doors which will have to stand closed. There are things done by others with easier codes which we know must not be done by us. At times it seems as if the way of faith were meant for some other kind of world than this. And the effort to take it means the loss of much that life seems to offer.

When this mood comes down on us, ways of escape are not far to seek. Doubts of the truth of Christianity begin to tempt us. The theories of the skeptic become plausible. It would be easy just to accept these views, and be free from the burden of belief and the demands of loyalty to Christ. For many people unbelief is only a way of escape. It is a way of accepting deliverance.

There is a sure way through this temptation. It is to remind ourselves that faith must always bring its burdens and difficulties. These are part of the price of loyalty. We must remember also those who have withstood to the death. Above all, we must think again of him who endured and accepted the Cross, refusing deliverance. As we think of these we know that there is no other honorable way. We know, as we look into the face of Christ, that those who follow him have even now the "solid joys and lasting treasure." We know that to follow him fully is to find life to the full, whatever the price. To stand fast, whatever it brings, is to have the joy that nothing can take away. When the sacrifice begins and is accepted, the springs of real joy are unsealed within us. For the pain of loyalty to him is the sharp tool which God uses to make our hearts tender to His most intimate love.

XXVIII

THE SKELETON IN THE CUPBOARD

*"Behold, the king had sack-
cloth within upon his flesh."*
2 KINGS 6: 30

THERE could be few stranger figures in the world
than this king of Israel. The city was besieged. The
iron grip of famine held it fast. It could not be long
before the enemy broke in to make an end. Mean-
time the king walked the streets in the purple and
fine raiment that ancient kings wore. But one day,
when some appalling horror made him tear his garments in despair, sackcloth peeped out. And sackcloth, in those days, was the sign of mourning or
penitence. They found that he was wearing sackcloth within.

If we let that picture touch our imagination for
a moment or two, it will suggest one or two things
to us about ourselves and one another.

For one thing, does it not remind us of the fact
that surface impressions are often wrong? There
are many around us whose outward circumstances
show little trace of suffering or trouble. We think
of them with envy perhaps. Or we make hard judgments about them. They have little to trouble them,

we think. If only they knew what we had to bear! But if we knew all, we might find that they had a secret grief or burden of which the world knows nothing. There is a skeleton in the cupboard. This rich man has all he wants. He lives in security and ease. But behind scenes he is carrying a load of anxiety that makes his days a weariness and his nights a horror. It may be that his only child is a cripple or his son has gone wrong. Or perhaps he is the victim of some physical weakness that takes away the savor of life. Life has infinite ways of hurting us. They may all be God's ways of making us humble and suppliant. But most people have their secret troubles of which the world never gets a hint. A brave smile may cover some unhealed wound of grief. Exciting pleasures may be an escape from the shadow of secret remorse. Hawthorne gives us a picture of a clergyman wearing a face of calm before his fellows and pleading with them about their sins. But in his own room he wrestles with an un-confessed and unforgiven sin that gives him no rest.

We little know the secret hearts of other people. If we knew all, someone says, we would forgive all. In any case, it is a warning against hasty judgments. Most of us can recall with shame some instances where we have wronged others in this way. We thought, and perhaps said, hard things about them. Then one day the truth came out and we found how shallow and cruel our criticism had been. Was it not this that Christ had in mind when He forbade us to judge one another? We do not know enough about the secret temptations and difficulties of others to give a verdict. There may be smiles or gaiety without, but sackcloth within.

There may be various motives for this reserve, of course. We may not want others to know our trouble because we are ashamed of the weakness. Or the forced courage or gaiety may be a way of escape. But there is often something brave about putting a cheerful face on things. It is good, at all events, not to give way to self-pity and to ask for sympathy. That is a common temptation. We tell our troubles so that others may give us their pity. We rather like to be known as a martyr. We want to get full value for our difficulties. Self-pity is a morass, and talking about our troubles is a way into it.

This does not mean that we must always keep a still reserve. But talking of our troubles may lead us to exaggerate them. It may make them harder to bear. But what is worse, it always adds to the trouble of the world. This king was not wearing fine garments to keep up appearances. He was doing it in order not to add to the gloom of life for the rest. He was whistling to keep up the courage of others. There is something fine about that. The right thing to do with a secret trouble, if we tell it to anyone, is to tell it to a friend who can be trusted

148

not to make us flabby with sympathy, but to help us to face it with courage. Best of all, it is to tell it to God and find His strength and healing in it. Most of us know how the oyster gets its pearl. A little bit of sand gets into its tender and sensitive heart. It sets to work to secrete the substance which will soften the friction and enable the painful intruder to lie easily in its heart. The result is a pearl.

But that hidden sackcloth had another meaning. It revealed the king's deep sympathy with his people. Perhaps they thought he did not care. But all the time he was feeling with them, though he kept a brave face on it. That secret sympathy with others is the quality of all who would lead or help their fellows. Someone says there are two kinds of people in the world, "those who would boss others and those who would understand them." It is this understanding of others that draws us together. Bridges of fellowship in the outer world will grow when we have built those bridges within.

There often seems very little that we can do to put wrong things right. We think of the slums or of unemployment and a dozen other ills of society. We feel so helpless that we may give up the problem and do nothing. But at least we ought always to feel with those who suffer. We ought to enter into the troubles of the slum-dweller or the out-of-work. We should never let ourselves live in peace. Their needs ought to create a tension in our souls that is never relaxed. It is from this hidden, sensitive sympathy that the power to change things will come.

Dr. Schweitzer says, "Reverence for life will not allow me to appropriate my own happiness. It refuses to allow me to banish my uneasiness." Was not this how Christ went through the world? He knew how to meet life with courage and joy. But all the time his heart was sore with the pain and sin of the world. Deep in his soul the world had already printed the mark of the Cross. It was this hidden link with men that made him the medium of God's love.

XXIX

THE THINGS THAT ARE VITAL

*"That ye may approve
things that are excellent."*
Phil. 1 : 10

In his version, Dr. Moffatt has given a new meaning to the words of St. Paul. It is that they may have "a sense of what is vital." Life is full of a multitude of things. There are things to do, to believe, to suffer, and to enjoy. Some of these are important. Many of them are trivial. They have no real effect on our lives. They do not matter much one way or the other. We can waste a good deal of time and energy if we do not have the sense of what is vital.

The success of life depends on this knowledge. A good business, for instance, can be ruined if the man who manages it does not know the things that make for success. We may study a great subject and make little of it if we do not see what are the main facts or principles. We may even read the New Testament and find it colorless unless we realize what are the vital things in the life or message of Christ. We may teach a Sunday-school class,

or even run a church, and accomplish nothing, if we
have not the sense of what is vital.

It is the same with the happiness of life. Things
happen to us that for the moment cloud our sky and
dull our happiness. But a week afterwards we know
that our anxiety was needless. The things we wor-
ried about were not really worth our notice. But
other things passed almost unnoticed, and one day
our eyes were opened and we found that in these
were wells of joy we had missed. It is tremendously
important to get a sense of proportion. We need to
learn to see life in its true perspective. One of the
most fruitful prayers we can make for ourselves is
that we may have the sense of what is vital.

This is true in every region of our life. But the
first place to make sure of it is in meeting life itself. Some of us go through life disillusioned and
disappointed. We have fixed our ambitions and
hopes on the wrong things. Most of us think we
know what happiness is, and how the ingredients of
it are made up. So we try for comfort or pleasure,
and at the end we find that happiness has eluded us.
Some of us think that the vital thing in life is money.
We use every means to get it. Perhaps we get it,
but it does not satisfy. We have grasped the shadow and missed the substance. Or perhaps we do not
get money, and we feel that life has been a failure.
We say that life is a lottery with many blanks and
few prizes, and we feel sore at heart that it has

cheated us of its golden promise. Or, what may be worse, we grow bitterly envious of those who seem to have been successful. The trouble is that we have failed to distinguish between what is useful or pleasant and what is vital. Some things are valuable but not vital. We can have the real satisfaction of life without them. Whatever our circumstances, this is a world where the best, in the true sense of the word, is open to all. When the Psalmist said that the Lord is good to all, he was right. But there is one condition. We must have the sense of what is vital and fix our minds on that.

The vital things in life are very few. Most people looking ahead might dispute this. In our youth, when the world is opening out its treasures, we have large ideas of what we need for the fullness of life. The more we get the more we desire. But as the years go on and we look back, we know that the real things were few and simple.

One of the vital things in life is to have a task and to put our best into it. It may be very humble and limited. It may bring us little material reward. But our true happiness is in "something attempted, something done." It may be just caring for a home or doing a humdrum job. But the real satisfaction is in doing it with all our hearts. There was a well of real joy in the heart of the man who, as the *Aquitania* first went down the Clyde, said to a friend,

"It is something to have put rivets into a boat like that."

Another of the vital things is friendship. Human relationships at their best are a well of happiness. At times we forget this. But as the years go by and it may be death has come to some we love, we know that every chance we took of showing affection or doing a kindness was something gained in vital living. Henry Drummond had enjoyed most things. But his own confession was that the high moments of his life were those in which the Spirit of Christ had impelled him to some act of human service.

The spirit in which we face life is another vital thing. We may have had troubles to meet and misfortunes to face. These may seem to have destroyed the possibility of happiness. But we discover, when we face them bravely, that that spirit was the important thing, and not the circumstances themselves. Something is won for us, through meeting difficulties in the right spirit, that can enter our lives by no other door. The real things are what have been won for character from trouble, and not the difficulties which trouble brought.

But the most vital thing in life comes into it through faith. Prayer is to the spirit what breathing is to the lungs. Faith in God puts into the atmosphere of life what is as vital to the soul as oxygen to the body. "I had fainted unless I had believed." That was the Psalmist's confession. Many of us faint and do not know the reason. We are peevish, ill at ease, perhaps depressed. It is because we have not realized that contact with God is vital. Religion is not an extra. It is the deepest necessity of life. It gives foundations to our world on which alone it can rest. It makes the trivial act of duty or service a stone in God's eternal building. It opens into our love a perennial spring that nothing can dry up. Every day we are meeting things that offer us the chance of fullness of life. Let us begin each day by asking God to give us the sense of what is vital.

XXX

OUR UNCONSCIOUS INFLUENCE

"Then came Peter, and went into the sepulcher.
. . . Then went in also that other disciple."
JOHN 20: 6, 8

THESE words describe how Peter and John visited the empty grave of Jesus. The news that he had risen was so astounding that they ran. John was there first. But at the door he hesitated, shrinking back. Perhaps it was only fear, the eerie feeling that the open grave must have brought. But Peter, coming up behind, dashed through the doorway. "Then went in also that other disciple."

Peter had given him, of course, just the stimulus he needed. But he did not think of influencing John. He thought of nothing except finding out the truth about Jesus. It meant everything to him that he should have risen. He had nothing else in his mind but to make sure that the astounding news was true. He just went on in his headlong love. But all the same, he was giving John the lead he needed to take him across the threshold of the new world.

The incident brings to mind the fact of our influence on one another. Most of us do things at times because others do them. They also do things

156

because we do them. Example is a stimulus to action. Friends tell us of books they are reading; we read them, too. Someone describes a holiday in an attractive place; we make up our minds to go. Instances can be multiplied. Hints, suggestions of one kind or another, are always passing from life to life, like seeds blown from one garden into others round it. We cannot escape this influence. We have each this power of affecting and being affected by others. Our very presence in a company may make a difference in directing talk or discussion. The more we like one another the greater is the power of this influence. Friendship opens a door into the heart through which our friend may pass at will.

How far can we control our influence on others and theirs upon us? How much ought we to try? We can at least keep a guard on the influence which others have upon ourselves. There are some whose effect on those around is a subtle lowering of ideals. The big things of life become cheap and small when they are near. The atmosphere becomes morally relaxing. We feel less like prayer when we have been in their company. The Christian way begins to seem a kind of foolishness. We should be on our guard against the infection of people like that.

But we must consider our influence on others in certain things at least. Some kinds of conduct may be lawful for ourselves. So, at least, we may feel. But there are others to whom these things are a

157

strong temptation, or a vice from which it is a struggle to keep clear. Our example may be the deciding point. It may carry them over the line on one side or the other. We have our responsibility for what we put into the atmosphere of ideals which everyone is breathing. Each of us is a link between others and God's power and love. Other people wait for our lead without knowing it, and most of all in taking the way of Christ. They are held back by fears, perhaps, or by mistrust of themselves. Our stand for Christ may decide them to come in. The fact that we pray may induce them to begin. We can be quite sure there is at least one who is depending on us in this way. Each of us may be the key to a new spirit in our home, our business, our church. There are places where God means us to take the lead. If we do, others will follow.

But there is a point to be remembered. Most influence is unconscious. We do not know that we are affecting others, or even what it is we say or do that affects them. Peter did not know his influence on John. Moses did not know when he came down from the mount that his face was shining. He was unconscious of any radiance. But the people saw it, and felt the power of this spiritual quality. It is this unconscious influence which really affects others, whatever we may say or do. It is the power of our hidden selves that makes its mark. We have all heard the saying, "What you are speaks so loud that

I cannot hear what you say." We have all felt this
at times about people. They tried to influence us,
but there was something in their spirit that canceled
out all their good advice. It might be said that
while we are speaking, some things are heard and
some are overheard. There are overtones and under-
tones in every conversation. It is these that influence
people. If what we say and what we are agree,
our influence may be strong. But it is the unconscious influence we must keep in mind

Every preacher or Sunday-school teacher should
think about this. While we exhort people, what is
it that is really speaking behind our words? Is it
hidden pride, or secret ambition, or the voice of our
own defeat? If we are parents, it is our unconscious
influence about which we should question ourselves.
What is really getting home in our counsel or advice?
What are the young people overhearing? What
is it in us that is really affecting them? Christianity
cannot be taught, it has been said; it must be caught.
It certainly cannot be taught unless through the
teaching there is the goodness that is infectious with
Christ's spirit.

How can we secure this unconscious influence?
We cannot do it by effort. But we can keep ourselves
close to God. We can keep open to His Spirit so
that He can make us clean from pride and fear and
lovelessness. We can seek to be utterly real within, remembering that our influence comes from what

159

we truly are. If we are honest and real with Christ in our own life, we need not fear about our influence on others. For all effective influence is the influence of His Spirit. Our speech may be blundering and our life full of faults. But He dwells in the heart that loves Him, and He cannot be hid.

XXXI

STANDING ON OUR FEET

"And he said, Son of man, stand upon thy feet, and I will speak unto thee."
EZEK. 2: 1

THIS was God's first word to the prophet Ezekiel. The vision of God had burst on his soul and he had fallen prostrate on his face in the dust. This humbling is always the result of coming face to face with God. But so long as a man lies there, he can be of little use to God. For even He can do nothing with a man who just lies on his face. God's first word to him therefore was a call to stand on his feet.

There is an idea that true reverence demands this posture of self-abasement. Those who have seen in the East the Mohammedan spreading his prayer mat and bowing down to the earth before the might of Allah are impressed by this devotion. It rebukes our Western pride and self-sufficiency. We can all learn from it. But it is very incomplete. True reverence is something more than this subjection of the spirit before God's might and majesty. It is the adoration of what is perfect in goodness and love. It will quicken us into active service and consecration. It will make us ready to be commanded by

God. It is the attitude of a soldier at attention. God wants us alert and eager, with all our powers on the altar, to be kindled by His flame. The saints of the Bible walked with God and talked with Him. They were the friends of God—not merely His subjects or His tools. Communion with Him needs all our powers of thought and imagination and will. He bids us stand on our feet and He will speak with us.

There are special times in which we need this rousing call. We need it when we are most conscious of our sin and failure. Such times of humiliation must come to us, if we are honest with truth. When we see God in all the glory of His love and goodness, the heart goes out of us. Our pride is deflated; our self-sufficiency is gone. "Now mine eye seeth thee," said Job after a long time of perplexity. "Wherefore I abhor myself and repent in dust and ashes." It is only on this foundation that God can build. But just then He speaks, and His word is of forgiveness. That is what it means to stand on our feet. It is to accept His forgiveness and cease groveling in the dust of our own futility or failure. He bids us rise up to begin again with Him. That is the only word that will put strength into us when we really see ourselves in God's light. Thinking of the good we have done will not avail. Making excuses for ourselves will not patch up our ruined self-respect. We can never take our place in God's Kingdom except as men whom He has forgiven. But His forgiveness will set us on our feet, for it is a call to the fullness and freedom of a new life.

We need this word also in the hour when life has disheartened us. Most of us know something of the crippling power of circumstances. It may be that sickness has taken from us the health we once had. We may have to face life physically limited. Or it may be that sorrow has invaded our home, and it looks as if life would never be the same again. There is a great temptation, in these circumstances, to give way to a mood of continuous depression. We fall on our face, like Ezekiel, and lie there. Some people call this the mood of resignation. They think it is one of the cardinal Christian virtues. When suffering comes they bid themselves or others to be resigned to the will of God. They try to cultivate submission. But they never recover the joy of life. They pass their days with a spirit from which all zest has gone. If resignation is a virtue, it is one of the unloveliest. But it is not a virtue. It is only halfway to it; and to settle down in this halfway house is to find it a very damp and unhealthy dwelling for the spirit.

There is a better thing than resignation. It is acceptance. It is to take the circumstances from the hands of God as the place in which we are to do His will. For the will of God is not our circumstances; it is the thing He wants us to do there. His call to us is to get up from the dust of self-pity or de-

163

jection. He has something for us to do, and we will find it when we are alert and ready for His call. His word to us in the pit of trouble is to stand on our feet.

Over fifty years ago a young man of twenty-five, with brilliant prospects before him and the joy of life in his veins, was suddenly blinded in a shooting accident. For some time he was numbed, though he tried to hide his depression. Letters from friends came by every post, all bidding him be resigned to the will of Providence. But none of these helped him. One day, however, he received a letter from his old tutor in Cambridge. It began with sympathy, but after a little the tone changed. "It will be your own fault," he said, "if this trouble does not bring some alleviation. The evil that has fallen upon you will lose half its terrors if regarded steadfastly in the face, with the determination to subdue it as far as may be possible." Then he went on to suggest a course of study, and to assure the stricken man that this blow must not hamper his career. It was the challenge he needed. It was the call to stand on his feet. The result was that he made a brave acceptance of his lot as his post of service. The joy of life came back. In a few years Henry Fawcett had become a Professor in Cambridge. In later years he was Postmaster-General in the Government of the day.

Are there some of us whom life has wounded

164

badly? We can be sure that God has not left us. His face may be hidden because ours is in the dust. But He is near. If we will listen, His challenge will come to us. "Have courage. Stand on thy feet, and I will speak with thee." What He will say to us then will open a new chapter which He and we will write together.

XXXII

THE MANAGEMENT OF MEMORY

"Forgetting the things that are behind."
Phil. **3: 13**

Memory is one of our greatest gifts. How precious
it is can be seen from the sadness that comes over us
when, with advancing years, it begins to fail. It is
even more wonderful than we realize. For we are
assured by those who study the mind that nothing
is ever quite forgotten. All that has made an impression on us passes into a secret pool within the
mind and stays there. Some things float on the surface and stare at us. Some things sink a little out of
sight, but are easily brought to light. Some, again,
sink to the bottom of the pool and lie there hidden.
But they make their influence felt. Their sweetness
or their bitterness steals through the mind and colors
our thinking. The things that are behind whisper
to us out of the past. They bring to us a quiet happiness or they stir in us a curious uneasiness, though
we may not know whence these feelings come. A
good deal of our conduct could be explained if we
knew exactly what lies buried in that pool of memory.

Nothing in life needs to be managed more care-tully than memory, for nothing can hurt us or hinder us more than this stored-up past. St. Paul knew that. He saw the Christian life as a kind of race, with himself as the runner. His success depended on keeping his eyes on the goal and the prize. He dared not waste energy by thinking of the past. No man can win a race who runs with his head looking over his shoulder. So St. Paul tells us that he forgets the things that are behind. He is thinking mainly of successes that have come to him, the work he was able to do for Christ, his victories over temptation. These are things to thank God for. But he will not dwell on them. He refuses to become complacent or self-satisfied. Rightly used, these memories may encourage us. They may spur us on. We can think of them and thank God and take courage. That is the right way to use them. But it is possible to let the mind linger on them in such a way that they prevent further progress. The good may become the enemy of the best. We can make a shell of our own success in which to curl up and go to sleep.

There are other things, unfortunately, in the pool of memory. These also have to be managed if they are not to hinder progress. Some things it is very hard to forget for long. Most of us have experiences of mistakes and failures. We have all felt the hard knocks of trouble or the crippling blows of sorrow. These experiences can stay in the mind and make

167

unhappiness. They may fill us with a dull sense of resentment. They may come back into the mind and bring a feeling of humiliation. There are people whose life of faith has ended in a grave where they have laid to rest one whom they loved. After that, life lost its spring. The joy went out of their hearts. Others go limping through life tied to the memory of an old failure. There is a way of managing these memories so that they shall cease to cripple us. It is to open them up to the light of God's love. It is to take hold of the fact that He can use them for our good and that He is with us in them. No experience is ever useless or even hurtful if we put it into God's hands and are willing to let Him weave it into the pattern of our life. But first of all we must be willing to let Him shape the pattern, and cease grieving because that which we had planned for ourselves has been spoiled. That may be where we need to begin. It may be that we had planned our life on a scale that is selfish or shallow. And the best thing that could happen to us is that life should tear up the plan. If we are ready for God's plan, we can be sure that, out of the failure, the trouble, the sorrow, He can make something more beautiful than we had dreamed.

Another group of unhappy memories are those that come from our relationships with others. Our contacts with people at home and business are so close that we cannot wonder that there is sometimes friction and strain. Words may be spoken and things done that make us angry. In time the anger dies. But in its place there rises a steady current of resentment, like smoke from a smoldering fire. A secret grudge can affect our life in various ways. It stays in the mind and rankles. It makes us cynical, perhaps. It keeps us from being our best with those who have hurt us. It makes us unfair in our judgments. It may even keep us from being honest with truth. Many a man's politics, and even his religious opinions, have been twisted by a secret antagonism. Above all, it keeps us from prayer. The heart that is tethered to a grudge cannot rise freely into the clear air of God's love. That is why Christ bids us settle our differences before we take part in worship. If life is to be unhampered, we must learn how to manage these memories. The first thing to do is to acknowledge them, and then to hold them steadily in the light of the Cross. If we have taken our own sins to the forgiving stream of God's love at Calvary we cannot keep an unforgiving spirit. His love will cleanse our own wound of its poison. We may need to go further and confess our resentment to the person who has wronged us. That is a sure way to be rid of it. Whatever else may happen, we shall have peace. The sting will be gone. It may be also that in place of the friction we shall find a new and closer friendship.

But the darkest things in the pool of memory are

our own sins. Nothing can be so painful as a guilty memory. St. Paul knew this experience. In the background of his mind there were "remembered faces—dear men and women whom I sought and slew." Most of us have in our minds remembered faces of some we have hurt or vexed. Things we have done and said come back to the mind, especially when we are nearest God. For His Presence stirs the pool of memory, and the sense of guilt darkens the waters. What can we do with these memories? They cannot be put away and buried. They must be brought to the light. They must be opened up to God. But His forgiveness can cleanse them. His grace can wash out the stains. After that they remain, but only to bring back to us, with the pain, the wonder of His love. They become the spring of gratitude. The poison of fear and bitterness is gone. "All my memories are now free from dread," said Augustine when he had let Christ deal with his past. That experience can be ours. Through Him there is peace and freedom to go forward into a new day.

XXXIII

MISTAKEN SUPPOSITIONS

*"She, supposing him to be the gardener, saith
unto him, Tell me where thou hast laid him."*
JOHN 20: 15

MARY must often have blamed herself for the mistake she made on Easter morning. She had come to anoint the body of her Lord. She never dreamed that he might have risen. She took it for granted that he was dead. When she saw the figure of this Man in the garden, it was very natural that she should take him for the gardener. Perhaps her eyes were misty with tears and her mind confused.

But the point is that she took it for granted that he was dead. It is amazing how many mistakes we may make by taking things for granted. There are some things, of course, we ought to take for granted. If we put a flower into the earth we ought to take it for granted that it will grow. If we have fulfilled the conditions, we can trust it to nature. It is part of the happiness of home that we can take things for granted that are not so certain outside. We can take it for granted that people will understand us, will think the best of us and stand by us.

But there is a danger in taking everything for

171

granted. Those we love may be hungry for some token of affection, some sign of appreciation. We think we can be petulant and irritable just because we are with people who love us. Love has been deeply wounded or starved and has sometimes even died just because it was taken for granted.

There are some common suppositions that are very mistaken. We find some cases of this kind in the New Testament. One of them is this of Mary. She supposed that Christ was not there, and with that in her mind she nearly missed him. What if she had turned away and left the garden without speaking to him? She would have met the risen Lord, but not just then. Maybe she would have had to go through a further time of desolation. Do not we sometimes make the same mistake? We go on from day to day as if Christ were not here and the world were empty of his presence. We take it for granted that life can never be any better. We never expect from Christ any victory over fear or despair or defeat. That is how some Christian people really live. They listen to the old story. But it makes no music in their souls. It carries no thrill. It brings no sunlight. Their world is bounded by what they see. Is it not time we began to get rid of this heavy air of listlessness that often hangs around our hearts? The mood of expectation is part of a living faith. In that air of expectancy, prayer becomes real. It gets things done. God is able to work. If we took it for granted that he is waiting to meet us, to answer us, to go with us, would not life be a new thing?

There is a second case of mistaken supposition that was nearly fatal. The disciples were out on the lake one day when a storm blew up. Squalls of wind threatened the boat. They rowed with desperate energy, but got no nearer the shore. Suddenly, Christ appeared walking on the water. They saw him coming and were terrified. They supposed they had seen a ghost. They got into a panic which might have sunk the boat. But fortunately they listened when he spoke, and they realized that it was their Friend. Many people have been in that position about him, and many still are. Christ fills them with fear. That is why some have come to invoke the saints to intercede with him for them. But others are still full of fear when they think of him. They do not want him too near. They imagine that he will denounce them. Some are even afraid of the emotion which Christ may awaken. They are afraid he will make them unnatural if he comes too close; that he will lead them into making fools of themselves. How absurd it all is! He wants to give us his friendship. That is the big thing, and everything follows from that. Keeping away from him, we are keeping out of the reach of a Love that would make us strong and fearless and real. We really want to be natural, to be ourselves, to live life to the full. It is only he who can make this possible.

173

When we fly from him, seeking peace, it is really he whom we are seeking.

There is yet another mistaken supposition that is very common. It is to think that Christ is with us when, in fact, he is not. His parents once did that with him when he was a boy. They had taken him to Jerusalem, and when the time came for them to go home they set out. They took it for granted that he was with them somewhere among their friends. "They supposed him to be in the company." But it was a mistake. They had to go back a long way, back to the temple, to find him.

It is very easy to make a mistake like that. We may take it for granted that we are Christians and that we belong to Him, when in reality we are still living for ourselves. We may take it for granted that he is with us, when we are really following our own selfish plans, spending money as we like, using our time in our own way, seeking our own will. We may even take it for granted that he is with us in our Church fellowship when in reality we have none of his Spirit, and are merely carrying out a routine of service or worship. It is a great mistake to suppose that he must be in the company because we are doing Church work. Are we sure that we have invited him? Are we seeking his guiding? Is there anything in our fellowship that we cling to which may be keeping him out? We may need to go back to find him, back to the place of penitence and a real

174

surrender. Perhaps the first step to a vital religion is for us all to make sure that he is really with us, because we are with him in purpose and spirit. "Where two or three are gathered together in my name, there am I in the midst of them." That is his sure promise. But let us remember the condition. Are we sure that we are meeting and working in his Name?

XXXIV

OUR WANTS AND OUR NEEDS

"Do you want to be made whole?"
JOHN 5: 6

FEW of us would think of asking a man who had been a cripple for thirty-eight years if he wanted to be healed. But that was what Jesus did. A man had been paralyzed for half a lifetime. He had spent every day lying on his bed by a pool, waiting in vain for his turn to be immersed in the healing waters. It seemed a most pitiful case. But Jesus expressed no sympathy. He merely put to him this strange question: "Do you want to be made whole?"

No doubt there was a reason for the question. The man was probably one of those people who make their ailments an escape from life. If he were well, he would cease to be interesting to other people. He would get no sympathy. He would no longer be the center of the picture. He would have to carry his burden like other people. So, bit by bit, he had grown used to his condition. Jesus evidently penetrated his secret. The root of his trouble was in the will. Hence the searching question, "Do you want to be made whole?"

Whether he wanted it or not, there was no doubt

that he needed to be healed. But what we want and what we need may be two different things. We do not always realize this. One of the sad features of our time is the number of people who seek only what they want. Their one question about everything is, "Do I want it?" They never ask whether they need it. If they are asked to go to church, they will only consider whether they want it. If they do not want it, that ends the matter. It is supposed to be sufficient. This point of view is disastrous. We do not leave children to decide whether they want education. We insist on them going to school because they need it. A boy who goes into life seeking only what he wants instead of what he needs will make shipwreck of life.

But to decide about religion by our wants instead of our needs is tragic. A well-known minister tells how he found on a cheap bookstall a book about salvation, which was priced at twopence. He inquired the reason for its cheapness, and was told that no one wants salvation nowadays. "No one may want it," he replied, "but everyone needs it." That is the point. We may not want to pray or to find God's love. It does not appeal to us. But that does not dispose of the fact that we need it. We will not seek God, of course, till we want Him, till the sense of need comes home to us and becomes a cry from the heart. That is the problem with which every preacher of religion is faced. How can men and women become so conscious of their need that it becomes the thing they want?

Even those who know their need of God and His grace have periods when their sense of need becomes blunted. The world is too much with us. Life moves along smoothly without anything to jolt us out of the ruts we have made for ourselves. God becomes dim and shadowy. Prayer seems unnecessary. God has His own way of awakening us. Trouble comes, or the shock of misfortune, or some stinging moral failure. We see the chasm opening before our feet where the ground had looked so solid. It is His way of awakening us to our need of Him. The first meaning of trouble is to drive us to His breast. Even if we can see no more in it than that, there is a blessing in it. It has quickened our hidden need into a want. And behind that want which forces us to seek Him, there is a door that opens into His love.

But we need not wait for that to become conscious of the need that brings us to Him. We need only think of the world around us. The big fact that stares at us is that it is very sick and cannot cure itself. There is no one to put it into the pool. The efforts made by statesmen and others to mend things are but tinkering with a house whose foundations have given way. Only the Spirit of Christ can deliver from the fear and hate that are paralyzing us. But how can he find his way into the world? Only as he finds his way into us. We flatter ourselves when we say that if everyone were like us all would be well. But would it? Have we in our own hearts none of these fears, and none of these hatreds and suspicions? A little self-examination will make us silent. It may bring us face to face with our own need of salvation.

But the most direct way is to keep our hearts open to Christ. He keeps us alive to our need of him. His light shatters our self-complacency. That is one reason why he has been so deeply hated and so dearly loved. He wakens needs we never can forget. He shows up "the plague of our own heart." When we keep close to him we realize that we need his salvation every day. We know that we dare not live out of his healing grace.

> They who fain would love Thee best
> Are conscious most of wrong within.

To be open to Him means more than keeping him before our minds. It means facing the tasks which he inspires. One big reason why we lose our sense of need is that we do not face things in his name that make us aware of our own insufficiency. If we are launching out on his service, we will know our own helplessness. We will find that without him we can do nothing. We will be meeting difficulties that are beyond our own strength. That is

179

one of the ways in which he keeps us ever humble and suppliant.

But there is more. For to see Him is to know that he loves us and wants us. That brings the sense of need. There are some who have this power over us. They show us glimpses of a friendship that makes us forever dissatisfied. They cross our path for a moment. Ever after, life is both richer for that moment and emptier. For a longing and a need have been awakened. It is like that with Christ.

> They who meet Him unawares
> Can never turn to earth again.

His friendship is the one thing that can fill the heart with peace. For we can rest in nothing which is not eternal. Why should we not be able to do without Him? That question is sometimes asked today by those who claim to feel no need. There is only one final answer. We are made that way. But those who have seen his love never ask it. They know only one thing. "We love him, because he first loved us."

XXXV

MORAL IMPOSSIBILITIES

"He saved others; himself he cannot save."
MATT. 27 : 42

Two of the most important words in the New Testament are "can" and "cannot." It is worth while to look at some of the things we *can* do. Christ puts many things within our power that were otherwise impossible. But it is also important to study the things we *cannot* do. There are some things which are morally impossible. Christ faces us at many points with a choice. We must be one thing or the other. We cannot have it both ways. We must make our choice.

For instance, He tells us that we cannot serve God and mammon. We must choose which of them will take first place in our reverence. Mammon is an ugly word. To see the thing pictured by G. F. Watts is enough to make us hate and loathe it. He shows us a huge, gross creature with brutal eyes seated on a throne, his hand on the neck of a woman and his foot on the body of a man. It is clear that we cannot worship both God and that. But that is what the money-spirit in all its forms means—the

181

spirit that puts material things first and makes these the standard of success. We can have money and yet worship God. We can have no money, and yet give the love of it first place in our hearts. But the danger is all the other way, and there can be no compromise. The soul that worships money and allows it to direct life can have no place for God. It is a moral impossibility.

Or, again, Christ said that if we do not deny ourselves we cannot be his disciples. That is very startling. The word "cannot" is absolute. Where self is not denied and put into the background in all its various forms, we cannot be his followers. He can teach us nothing. He can make nothing out of us. He can make no use of us. It is a moral impossibility. For his way will often conflict with our way. His ideas will often contradict our human wisdom. His plans will often be different from those we make for ourselves. The kind of person he would make of us may be very different from the person which in our own pride we have sought to be. Perhaps we had not realized his call for self-denial was so absolute as this. We had thought of it as a good thing, a very praise-worthy virtue, only to be attained by specially gifted souls or those who were deep in Christ's secret. As for ourselves, we had felt, like Professor James, that a little self-denial is a good thing to keep our spiritual lives in training. But to make a daily practice of it, to be always ready to put self behind us—that is what he asks as the price of any discipleship at all. "Christianity without tears" is a moral impossibility.

One of the most startling of these moral impossibilities was stated by Christ's enemies. It was meant for a sneer. They jeered at him, hanging so impotently on the Cross, while they recalled how his power had taken from others their pain, and rescued them from the deforming hand of disease. "He saved others; himself he cannot save." They were stating a fact. They were describing a moral impossibility. It was just because he saved others that he could not save himself. The price of his power to save us was his own journey down the dark valley. It was because he went through these gates of death that he could open them heavenwards.

There are so many ways of putting this amazing fact that language fails. Most of all, it makes us think of what it cost Him to win us from sin and selfishness. He had to carry the burden of it all, to set us free. Love, in his case, meant that he felt himself one with the human race. "In all their afflictions he was afflicted." That was literally true. In all the sins of men, in all their moral failures and tragic wrongdoing, He felt himself involved—he who had done no wrong. He knew the shame of men gone wrong, because he knew the love of God from which they had turned away. But he could not bring to them the awakening to it all, or the

183

assurance of forgiveness, except through this love that was one with them, and went all the way in suffering. There was no other method. To save himself and yet save men was a moral impossibility.

The same fact is true for us. It is a moral impossibility to help others in any real way without giving something of ourselves. It may often be a physical sacrifice. The tragic list of early deaths on the mission field is inevitable. They are part of the price that must be paid. Kipling sang of blood being the price of admiralty. It is the price of something much finer, but it is the price that must often be paid. The cost, of course, may not be in this physical coin. But if we are really to help people deeply, we must pay it in some form. In a real sense Christ was carrying the Cross all his days. For the people he helped took it out of him all the time. Virtue went out of him; he knew the drain of energy, the sacrifice of time, the mental strain that comes when we really put ourselves at the disposal of others. He knew the bitter pain of seeing those that he loved turn their backs to the light. Without that cost he could not have helped them.

It is the same with us and it is good to remember it. There are special times when we need to realize it. It may be that we are feeling the strain and the burden of some service we are doing. There are people whom we are trying to help, but they are costing a lot of trouble and time. There are others who disappoint us and are bringing us a good deal of pain. We are tempted, perhaps, to be a bit impatient, and to grudge the loss of time and energy. We may even pity ourselves, or be tempted to think of our self-sacrifice as a virtue. It is a good thing to remember that time and energy and sympathy are the inevitable price of saving others. There is no other method. We cannot have it both ways. We cannot live a life that is useful to the kingdom of God and one that never walks the way to Calvary. It is a moral impossibility.

We need to remember this particularly when our service is ineffective. Has it enough self-sacrifice in it? Do we give ourselves to others without reserve? Has our giving of money the mark of sacrifice? That may be why our service never reaches the point of power, nor gets through to the core of someone's need. It may be that we do not love enough to let God's love through to some hearts that are waiting for it. If we are to live in His way, we cannot save ourselves, our comfort, our ease, or our pride. But this saying needs another to make it complete: "He that loseth his life for my sake, shall find it." We can depend on that.

XXXVI

LETTING GOD TAKE THE STRAIN

"Consider the lilies, how they grow."
MATT. 6: 28

THIS is Christ's advice to those who are wearied with
the strain of life. One can imagine some people
smiling at the idea or even being irritated by it. It
may be that business is going down, and we do not
know how things may be with us next year. Or
perhaps we have a constant struggle to make ends
meet. How can we be expected to imitate the lilies
with their carefree life in the sunshine? They have
no need to think or plan about meals, or clothing, or
a dozen other things. Could Jesus have been really
serious?

He is not saying, of course, that we need not work.
He knew what work was. He ran the business for
some years after his mother became a widow, and
he had the care of the family. It is not work he is
asking us to get rid of. It is worry. That is what
brings the strain into life, so that temper gets
fretted, and friction wears us out. Worry is anxiety
about things which are not in our control and which
God will take care of, if we let Him. It is the fear
about tomorrow, or about the results of our plans.

186

It is the load that comes on the heart when we think of all the ills that may happen to us or to our children. For all these, Jesus tells us, God provides. Our part is to face the task of today and leave the rest to Him. Would it not lift the strain if we took His advice and trusted God's care? It would not make us less efficient or less active. It would set us free to face our work with greater energy. For worry has no driving power. It is, in fact, a brake on the wheels. Christ offers a way of freedom from this strain. It is to trust God fully with all the things that are out of our power. There is more, of course, to be said on this matter than can be put into a few sentences. But at least there is a secret here by which strain may disappear. It is to get a fuller vision of God's care, and live in it. It is to let God take the strain. "If God so clothe the grass of the field, shall he not much more provide for you?"

There is a message here also about the life of the spirit. Why is it that some Christian people are so often gloomy? They seem almost afraid to be happy. There are people whose conversion has taken all the joy out of their lives. It seems to lay on them a burden of care about their own souls and those of others. It dries up the springs of laughter and brings a strain into their lives that was not there before. It is not that they are hypocrites. They may be very honest and earnest. In a recent novel, the writer portrays a woman whose father was a deeply

187

religious man. He forced on her the obligation of duty till it became a kind of obsession. "The anxious, brooding sense of duty, the terror of failing in it, were with her day and night." Life was one long strain after an ideal which she imposed on herself, but was never able to reach. Wherever she went she carried this strain with her, till the lives of others in her care were made wretched by it.

We can be sure that Christ does not mean us to live like that. He himself was so happy that all kinds of people welcomed his company. Yet he carried the burden of the world's redemption. His secret was that he was living day by day in absolute dependence on the resources of God. He knew that God was sufficient for all his deepest need. There are things none of us can do for ourselves. "Which of you, by worry, can add an inch to his stature?" A boy does not grow by thinking about it. He takes food and plays games and leaves his body to grow, like the lilies. It is the same with our spiritual lives. The growth of the soul is not in our hands. No amount of strain will add one virtue to character or produce one beautiful grace of spirit. No amount of striving will enable us to overcome one temptation. Whatever good there is in us is wrought by the Spirit of God, working in the secret places of the heart. We need to realize this fact and rest upon it.

Not what these hands have done
Can save this guilty soul.

188

> Not what this toiling flesh has borne
> Can make my spirit whole.

This is God's work in us and for us. "Not of the works of righteousness which we have done, but of his mercy he saves us." It is He and only He who saves.

This does not mean that we need make no effort, that we are not to pray or discipline ourselves. Christ bids us both watch and pray. But these things are to be done in the deep peace of a mighty dependence on God. Christ died to win us by his love into that forgetfulness of self that thinks only of him and seeks to do his will.

Ruskin says, "There is the evidence of ease about the great works of nature. When we look at them we do not say, 'There is a great effort there,' but 'There is a great power here.'" Is that what people say of us and our goodness? Do they look at our strained faces and say, "There is a great effort there"? Or do they feel that about us which makes them say, "There is a great power here"? What Christ asks of us is simple. "Keep yourselves in the love of God." Our prayer and effort will be to see his love and confide in it utterly.

> Then work Thy work in me
> As Thou Thyself hast wrought,
> And let my love the answer be
> To all Thy love has brought.

That is how the lilies grow. They live in the light. God's love does the rest.

189

XXXVII

THE NECESSITY OF FREEDOM

*"Stand fast therefore in the liberty
wherewith Christ hath made you free."*
GAL. 5 : 1

THE call to stand for liberty is one that thrills most
people. Freedom is too precious a gift to be given
away. We resent more than anything having our
liberty taken from us. We claim the right to order
our lives as we think best. We insist on being allowed to take our own way, even though we make
mistakes. Dan Crawford, in *Thinking Black,* tells
us that the prize of liberty to the slave is "the blessed
luxury of choice."

There are some things, of course, that cannot be
found without liberty. Character cannot be won
without it. A child which is kept in leading strings
will never grow up. People who are not free to
think for themselves will never have any real convictions of their own. One of the things that Christ
did was to set people free. "Where the Spirit of
Christ is," Paul tells us, "there is liberty."

But it is good to think a little about this liberty
which Christ brings. For it alone is the true kind
of liberty. It is not just the freedom to do as

we like. That is liberty of a kind. But when people claim only that kind of liberty they are on dangerous ground. If we look into it, we may find that in doing as we like we have really lost our liberty. For what we like may be something selfish. It may be only satisfying some appetite, or following some strong impulse of self-will, and that is a form of bondage. The liberty which Christ gives is the power to do what we ought. It is the freedom to do the right, to be our best. We are only free if we are able to do what conscience asks, and what the Spirit of Christ directs. That is what freedom is for. Many of us have roses in the garden, and we have just been pruning them. We have had some of the straggling shoots cut off. But why not let them be free? Why curtail the liberty of the little tree to spread in any way it likes? There is no difficulty in answering this question. The only true freedom for the tree is the freedom to become its best. All other freedom—the freedom to grow out in any direction—would hurt it. And the only freedom we should claim for ourselves is the freedom to be our best.

This means freedom to serve others. That is what Paul goes on to say. "Let not your liberty be an occasion for the flesh." Do not let it be an opportunity for self-indulgence or sin. "But in love serve one another." That is the liberty for which Christ has made us free.

But what is this liberty? It is the freedom from the power of anything that keeps us from being like Christ. For that is what our best is. It is what we should be if we were fully grown. He is the perfect pattern.

And what are the things that keep us in bondage? They are nearly all within ourselves. Prejudice is one of them. If we have prejudice, we cannot be impartial. We cannot think rightly or help other people fully. It is the hardest thing in the world to be natural with anyone against whom we have a prejudice. We take wrong meanings out of their words. We do not give them credit for their good actions. We suspect their motives. Our minds are apt to be full of these prejudices. Some of them come from the class in which we have been brought up. Some come from our love of the nation we belong to. Old wrongs keep poisoning the blood. Christ can break these bonds. He helps us to accept others and see them as God's children, whom He loves equally with ourselves.

Selfishness is another form of bondage. It is so natural always to ask how this or that is likely to affect ourselves. Sometimes we go no further, and because it is natural, we are apt to think it must be accepted. But Christ says "No." We can come to love others as we love ourselves, and when that kind of love comes, we find that we are the richer for it. Our true wealth is the wealth of our love.

192

Our true poverty comes from the narrowness of the self-centered heart. It is like living in a big house with a lot of empty rooms. God made us with plenty of room in our hearts because He wants us to fill them with other people.

Hate and pride are also forms of bondage. A good many people do not think so. But when we think of it, we realize that hate is a real burden to carry. It is a poison in our own hearts. It has its worst effects on the person who hates. Out in the garden we may find one day that a climbing convolvulus has twined itself round the stem of some healthy plant. If we did not know what its nature is, we might think it beautiful; but it is binding and choking the life of that plant round which it clings. Hate and pride are like that.

These things, and others like them, are the real bondage of life. It is from these that Christ sets us free. And when the bondage of them is broken we are really free, for we have liberty to do his will. We are free for his commands. We are ready for the tasks of love and service.

It is when we are free in this real sense that we know what liberty is. For us, no laws are irksome; there are none that we want to break. No call to service cramps our freedom; for that service is what we long to do. It may not always be easy to do what He asks. But every time we obey we are breaking some shackle. We are confirming our freedom. We are claiming our liberty. It may help us to remember this, in some hour when we are tempted to give way or to go back. It is our liberty in Christ which is at stake in the hour of temptation. For every moral failure helps to forge a chain. Therefore let us keep our liberty, and "be not entangled again in the yoke of bondage."

When St. Paul spoke of liberty in this letter, however, he was thinking of yet another kind of liberty. It was freedom from irksome restrictions on fellowship with Christ. The Jewish religion demanded of a man certain rites before he could be sure of God's fellowship. St. Paul had shown them that it becomes ours only through faith in Christ. He has done all for us that needs to be done to open the way to God. The whole wealth of the country of his love is open to us. No ritual of penance or works of our own are needed to win this gift. It is ours by the victory of his cross. This is our birthright in the gospel. It seems too good to be true. We find it hard to believe. Because of that there is danger lest we should let a morbid conscience bring us under the bondage of a religion of good works or one which puts a barrier of rites and ceremonies between us and the free grace of God. From this tyranny our forefathers freed us when they broke the shackles of priestcraft. Into this liberty Hugh Latimer stepped when he discovered that he could not win God's forgiveness but had only need to accept it. Into this liberty Wesley stepped when it came home to him that the love of God was His gift and could be received no other way. It is our most precious heritage. The gates of life are open to all, whoever they may be, whatever they have done. "Whosover will, let him come and take the water of life freely." That is the ringing message of the gospel. We must take our stand for this precious freedom. We must not close or let anyone close the gate which Christ has opened so wide. For this is the road to every other liberty.

XXXVIII

OUR REAL HANDICAPS

*"Therefore putting away all handicaps,
let us run the race set before us."*
HEB. 12: 1

ONE fact is clear from the New Testament letters.
These people took life very seriously. The pictures
in which they describe it reveal this fact. They
thought of it as a fight, or a race. It was not something merely to experience and enjoy. It was something to do, to accomplish, to win. St. Paul, looking back on his life, summed it up in this way, "I
have fought a good fight. I have finished my
course."

To be successful in accomplishing God's purpose
for us we must be prepared to be "all out." We
must put away all that handicaps us in the effort
to follow Christ. That is the point of this message, as Dr. Moffatt translates it. No man in his
senses would try to run a race with any needless
weight to carry. He gets rid of everything that
hinders him. He puts on the lightest clothing. He
trains his body so that it is free from any super-
fluous flesh. He leaves behind every needless burden that would handicap his strength.

But what are the real handicaps of life? That is what we need to be clear about. We are apt to think of them as things in our circumstances. Some people, for instance, are poor and have many disadvantages. They are apt to imagine that these make any real success impossible. Others are physically crippled. Accident or disease has taken from them some physical power. They feel their defect and may be discouraged. But are these things real handicaps? We have only to look around us to see what has been done by such handicapped lives. Countless people have had a hard time and few advantages, but in spite of them they have fought their way to a place of distinction. Many have gone through life maimed in some form, but in spite of it they have produced some of the finest work in every sphere of life. Milton was blind. Beethoven was deaf. John Keats was an invalid. Stevenson was a consumptive. The list is legion. St. Paul had what he called his "thorn in the flesh," and said so little about it that we do not even know for certain what it was. He prayed that it might leave him. But he could not get rid of it. The answer to his prayer was that God's grace was sufficient for him.

We say of these that they did great work in spite of their handicaps. Should not we rather say that it was because of them? Those who have had such handicaps and overcome them would say that they were a stimulus rather than a hindrance. They were

197

like the resistance in the electric bulb that makes the current burst into light. That was how they accepted them. We cannot always choose our circumstances, but we can always choose the spirit in which we shall meet them. Handicaps can quicken courage and endurance. They can develop hidden capacities. They can throw us back on God, whose grace is always sufficient for the task in hand. The real handicaps of life are not without but within. They are in the mind and the spirit. It is these that keep us from living the fullest Christian life and finding the fullest fellowship with others.

There is, for instance, the sense of grievance. It may be that someone has hurt us and we carry the wound in our heart unhealed. Or life has hit us hard and we resent it. We feel a rankling sense of injustice. Everything is embittered by it. We cannot get the full flavor out of the joys of life. There is always a cloud in the sky. We are not free to enter into the happiness of others. The channels of prayer are choked and the face of God is hidden.

Another handicap is the sensitiveness that is easily hurt. We are what is called touchy. We are depressed by criticism. We are unwilling to face unpleasant facts about ourselves or our work. There is a place for sensitiveness in life. We ought to be sensitive to the feelings of others, and sensitive above all to evil. But to be afraid to face any kind of criticism, and to be ready to see slights, is only a

198

form of pride. That is always a defect. "No man ever had a pint of pride that was not a disadvantage to him." God can teach the proud nothing. There were many places on the road to the Celestial City where the Pilgrim was disciplined. One of those was the Valley of Humiliation. Till he had gone through that, and learnt his weakness and lost his pride, he was unfit for God's service. We have much to be grateful for, but nothing to be proud of. Nothing can handicap us on God's service like the unwillingness to face the truth.

There are things also that handicap us for fellowship. Some people are handicapped by a critical mind. They have a keen eye for what is wrong in others. That is good if we are really trying to help them. But we may see the faults of other people so clearly that we cannot see what is good. The result is that it throws up a barrier between us and them. Jesus had a keen eye for what was wrong in people. But it was the eye of love, and what he saw brought tears. But he saw also what was good. He saw the tiny flower of faith or purity, peering up among the weeds that choked it. And he touched it with a smile of encouragement that was like a ray of sunshine. The first step to fellowship is to put away the spirit of criticism, and in its place put the spirit of encouragement.

Or think of the handicap of our prejudices. Where these come from we cannot always trace.

Training and custom bring them. Most of us have them. We are suspicious of those of a different class or a different nation. We dislike certain people. The fault may be ours, not theirs. We may be looking at them through the eye of jealousy or suspicion that distorts what it sees. We have been told, of late, that scientists have discovered a combination of electric rays in which a man becomes invisible. There are currents of feeling in the mind that keep us from seeing others as they are. There are many who have unattractive ways but hearts of gold. But prejudice may keep us from seeing the gold amid the dust. These prejudices hold up fellowship. They are at the moment amongst the biggest barriers to the Kingdom of God.

Such things are the real handicaps of life. It is these and such as these we must get rid of, if we are to follow Christ's lead. It will help us to be done with them if we face them honestly, and confess them, and keep guard upon them. But the only final way is to take them into the presence of Christ. That is the real remedy. The secret of release is to keep in the full light of Christ. It is "looking unto Jesus." And this means looking with a prayer in our hearts. It means looking to him for help. And no man ever looks to him in vain.

XXXIX

WHY ART THOU CAST DOWN?

*"Why art thou cast
down, O my soul?"*
Ps. 42: 11

THERE are times in life when we ought to take ourselves to task. We fall into some mood in which
we need honest and faithful handling. A true friend
would do it for us, for a real friend is what Emer-
son called a "kind of beautiful enemy." It is the
business of a friend to be a foe to anything in us
which keeps us below our best. And the best thing
we can do in certain moods of gloom is to seek out a
friend whom we can trust and bid him be honest
with us. We do not know what real fellowship in
Christ can mean till we learn to be honest with one
another about our faults. "If we walk in the light,
we have fellowship one with another."

But we can take ourselves in hand. We can put
questions to ourselves. Some shadows creep on the
spirit unawares and for little apparent reason.
Others come with trouble or disappointment. It is
good to challenge ourselves. "Why art thou cast
down, O my soul?"

It may be that in these words the Psalmist is

only rallying himself, bidding his soul make a stand. How is it that one like you should give way to this mood? he seems to say. If we compare our lot with that of other people we should be ashamed of uttering one peevish word. The thought of our mercies would light the darkest night with stars.

But the best way of rallying our hearts is to think of our resources in God. Take a great Psalm like the 23d—the record of centuries of experience, "The Lord is my shepherd." Think what follows from that. "I shall not want. He leadeth me. He restoreth my soul." Moods have no influence on the unchanging fact of God's love for us. Even when they come through some blow or misfortune or defeat they cannot change His love. He is nearest to us when we need Him most. Mazzini compared the dark hours of depression to the storms that beat on the head of a traveler. He wraps his cloak around him more firmly and goes on. No change in the weather can alter the object of his journey or drive him from the road. This is a picture worth remembering. But there is something even better to remember. "Though I walk through the valley of the shadow, I will fear no evil; for thou art with me." No storm can deprive us of our Companion, though it may blind us for the moment to his presence. "Why art thou cast down, O my soul?"

But this question may be more than a rallying call. It may be a real question that we ought to

202

put to ourselves. Why is it that we are depressed? What has brought the gloom? It is sometimes as useful to probe the maladies of the soul as the sickness of the body. Why is it that this or that has depressed us so? What was it in reality that brought on the dark mood? There may be other roots for our despondency than can be found even in the actual trouble.

Some people, for instance, cannot get over a great sorrow. The heart seems to have gone from life, and all its skies are gray. They cannot lift their heads. There is a shadow that covers everything. The spring is out of their step. Perhaps the root of this trouble is that their love has twined too closely round the one who has gone. This may seem a strange thing to say. It suggests that people can love too deeply. Indeed, some have said, in an effort to explain the death of a child, that God took him away because they loved him too much. But that is not the situation. They were too dependent on the one who has gone. They have never found that fellowship with God in which nothing we have loved can ever be lost. No human love in itself can bring our spirits final peace. It needs His fellowship to give love the quality that can deeply satisfy our hearts. And it needs His love to give our love security in a threatening world. If sorrow has brought us into a gloom that will not lift, it may be we are like a plant whose roots are feeding on the

203

surface. We have not found the deeper springs through which the joy of life and the joy of love can never wither.

Or our gloom may come from the fact that we are self-centered. We expect that life should always treat us tenderly and with respect for our feelings, and it has not come up to our hopes. We have always done our best. We have tried to help others and to take the straight road. So we tell ourselves. We did not deserve what has happened to us. There is resentment and perhaps a bit of hurt pride in our gloom. That is what makes it so bitter and keeps it breeding poison in our hearts.

There is only one way out of this kind of gloom. It is to begin to take life from God, seeking only to meet it in His way. That is the secret of resilience of spirit. Those who have it may be beaten, but they are never crushed or broken. They have a quiet way of rising above the waves that look as if they would sink them utterly. Their secret is that they are never concerned with themselves or their feelings, but with what they ought to do and how they can make the best of it. They never settle down in the Slough of Despond. They look for the solid places on which they can set their feet. They are not absorbed in themselves.

So let us ask the question when the shadow falls, "Why art thou cast down, O my soul?" It may be that what we need is to get our feet fixed on the rock of the purpose of God, instead of seeking the primrose path of our own pleasure or self-will. It may be it is sin that brings the shadow. We have a lack of inner resources and of peace because there is a secret estrangement from God. But however it may come, the gloom of the spirit is on the way to be scattered when we look up from our depression, and ask, "Lord, what wilt thou have me to do?" For then our face is to the light. And then, like Bunyan's Pilgrim in the Slough of Despond, we will find held out to us the mysterious hand of one called Help, to pull us out and set us on firm ground.

XL

THE TEST OF PROGRESS

*"Grow in grace, and in the
knowledge of Jesus Christ."*
2 PET. 3: 18

PROGRESS is an idea we have grown very fond of.
We are always seeking to make progress in various
directions. We scan the child's report from school,
looking for progress. We read reviews of the past
year describing progress. We feel the need for getting on. In every way, we like to think, the world
grows better and better.

The urge to make progress is natural. We have
come to realize that if the world is not getting better
it will be getting worse. The same is true of ourselves. "Who ceases to be better," said Cromwell,
"ceases to be good." That is true of life all round.
Gardens left to themselves go back to the wild. If
we are not trying to make headway, we shall be
drifting. It is as if we were set to climb a moving
staircase by the descending stair. We can only do
it if we are strenuous enough to overcome the downward movement. That is like life. But one thing
we have discovered. There is no stream of progress

206

which will carry us along. That is an illusion. Drifting is always downward.

But what is the test of progress? Our inventions only add to our physical power. The telescope increases the range of our eye; the wireless, the power of the ear. The huge machines that fill our factories increase the power of our hands; our motor cars, the speed of our feet. But these inventions merely add to our physical powers. They add nothing to our moral stature. The only real test of progress is within. What kind of people are we becoming? Are we growing kinder, gentler, purer, more unselfish? Are we learning the community spirit? Do we find it easier to live with others in the home, the nation, the world? Are we growing the kind of nature which will enable us to work together and rise out of the enmities and rivalries and jealousies of the jungle? No other progress is real. The Kingdom of God is not invention and material power; it is peace and joy in the Holy Spirit. The true growth is within ourselves. "Grow in grace, and in the knowledge of Jesus Christ."

Growing in grace is one form of real progress. What grace means is difficult to put into a word. It means likeness to Christ. It means those virtues that spring, like flowers, from the stem of his love. Are we growing in considerateness toward others? That is one test. Do we think more of them and their needs, and less of our own plans and wishes?

207

It is in the home that this grace should find its flowering place. Are we less insistent on our own demands, and more concerned with helping one another? We often misuse the privilege which home gives us of being our natural selves. The side which we show to those we love is often our worst. We grumble about our troubles. We take no care to hide our irritations. We fail in the courtesies of love that we sometimes show to those outside. It is hardest, perhaps, to be a Christian at home, just because no one will judge us there. We depend too much on the understanding charity and the long-suffering patience of wife or husband. That is why home life can be the most revealing test of what we really are. Are we growing in the graciousness of love at home?

Or what about our attitude to those who serve us in the workshop or the office? Business, in these days, brings a big strain. There are worries that fret the temper. Those under us may be watching our faces in the morning to see what mood we are in. They also have their troubles, but they must hide them. Are we growing in the grace that can bear with quietness the upset of our plans or the failure of some business deal? "All the great Christian personalities have one outstanding quality," says a writer. It is the quality of love. No one can mistake it. Are we growing in the spirit of love? Are we dwelling more and more deeply at the fountainhead of the grace that can change and soften us? For only in the grace of Christ can we find the secret of graciousness.

True growth is also growth in the knowledge of Christ. That does not merely mean the knowledge about Christ. So far as that is concerned, we know only what his disciples have to tell us. Knowledge of Christ means something deeper. It means the knowledge of him as personal Friend, entering into our lives with guiding and challenge. We can know him as a power that inspires and comforts. We can know his ways with us, how he would have us bear ourselves in trouble or difficulty. To know him means to enter into all that he means for our life. We cannot test our progress here by looking within. One test would be our interest in prayer and our joy in it. Another would be our eagerness to listen for the things he can say to our hearts about our daily life and its problems. Are we becoming more and more dependent on him? Do we find an increasing vitality in his words?

The best test of all is whether He becomes more precious to us as the days go on. We grow as he becomes more and more the center of our world. Or is he drifting out of our world—a far-off figure whose spirit haunts the hills of Galilee, but has no place in the streets of London or the office or shop in Birmingham? We can depend on it that if we get to know him better we shall be growing within.

No one can live near to Christ without becoming like him. Our progress, in real things, comes through what his spirit does within us to cast out self, to subdue the temper and the pride. As we come to know him, he gives us his grace. As we behold him and are obedient, we are changed. We may not know it. We may see little sign, or even only have a deeper consciousness of how far short we come. But his love, as we are open to him, will make our souls a mirror in which he can reflect himself. That is true progress. As our vision of Christ grows clearer our likeness to him will grow deeper. The end of it, as we are told, is that we shall have perfect vision and attain perfect likeness. That is the goal to which he seeks to lead us. It is the hope of that which can sustain us in all our striving. We know that when he shall appear, we shall be like him, for we shall see him as he is.

XLI

TWO KINDS OF SORROW

"Godly sorrow worketh repentance; but the sorrow of the world worketh death."
2 Cor. 7: 10

Most of us would say that there are many kinds of sorrow. St. Paul tells us there are two. He calls them "godly sorrow" and "sorrow of the world." How are they to be distinguished? For they are very different. The real question in regard to sorrow is not why it should have come, or why it should have come to us. It is what effect it is producing on us. We find it very hard at times to realize this. We are naturally concerned, if we can, to avoid it. We think we are happy if we do, and count ourselves unfortunate if we cannot. But the real question is how we bear it, if it comes, and what we get out of it. We can make spiritual capital out of our sorrows. Or we can see in them nothing but bitterness and loss. We can find in them the joy that comes through tears. Or we can find in them only what hardens and embitters the spirit.

Sorrow may take many forms. We generally apply the word to the grief that comes through bereavement. That is, perhaps, the most common form of it. But there are other forms. There is the sore heart that misfortune brings. We have worked long and hard to make a competence or build a business, and, through some turn of the wheel of fortune, all we have gained is lost. That is not an easy stroke to bear. There is also the sorrow of broken friendship. Misunderstanding or jealousy may bring estrangement. That makes a very deep wound. There is the sorrow, too, that comes when someone we love goes wrong or breaks our trust or disappoints our cherished hopes. These may be deeper sorrows than death brings. Or, again, there is the sorrow that is brought by our own failure or sin. To meet with trouble, and to know that it is our own fault, is a bitter experience. When selfishness or pride has done damage that we can never repair in this life, the memory of it can eat into the soul like a cancer.

Such experiences come to us all. They may become either godly sorrow or the sorrow of the world. It all depends on how we face them. We can put them into God's hands. We can ask Him what message He has for us in the dark valley. Dr. Moffatt translates the phrase "godly sorrow" as "the pain which God is allowed to guide." What word has God for our souls in the sad situation? If we listen, we can find it. For there is no situation whatsoever in which the trouble that smites us may not become God's messenger. He may give us a

212

word of rebuke. He may speak to us through our loss about the real things of life. He may show us our need for His fellowship, which perhaps we had been losing. He may rally us with courage. He may call to us through some estrangement for the forgiving spirit that can heal a break so that the friendship becomes stronger than before. He may rebuke us and bring us to our knees through the sense of shame. He can make the fire of remorse a cleansing flame. In that case, our sorrow will work repentance. It will draw us to Him. It may bring us back from some path of self-will where we had been wandering.

But our sorrow may become the sorrow of the world. It may embitter us. It may harden the heart instead of breaking it to let Him in. That happens to many people. They go through life after some blow, stony-hearted. The springs of their compassion are frozen. The roots of faith are withered. The reason is that they have not taken their trouble to God to let Him speak through it. They have kept it from the love that would have taken the poison out of the wound.

The sorrow of the world has various forms. One of them is baffled ambition. That may be the real soreness in loss or misfortune. There is an unforgettable picture of Napoleon walking with bowed head in his inland prison of St. Helena. What thoughts were festering in his mind we do

not know. But part of the sadness on that face was
baffled ambition. It may be the same with us when
failure or misfortune comes. Our cherished plan
has been defeated. We let it vex us and sadden us,
and perhaps think we are justified in grieving. We
do not let it criticize our ambition and set us on
the road to find some higher thing to live for. It is
the sorrow of the world.

Or it may take the form of wounded pride. This
is much more common than we imagine. It often
comes through some wrong that others have done
us. We may think it is their sin which has grieved
us, but in reality it may only be our pride which is
hurt. This hurt pride is often mingled with other
sorrows. We may imagine we are grieving deeply
because of a bereavement or some hardship that
makes life difficult. But behind it there is resentment that *we* should have been so treated. We feel
we have not got our due. We are humiliated. Our
self-love has been wounded. It is this which may
be putting the real poison into the wound, and
keeping us from finding the comfort of God.
The grief that springs, in part, from wounded pride
is what George Eliot calls "the sorrow that has no
balm in it."

But another form of it is that which comes
through sin, where conscience is unawakened. Sin
brings sorrow because it gets us into trouble. It
brings the sad harvest of physical evil or business

214

failure. We may grieve over it, but the grieving may only be for the consequences, not for the sin. The prodigal knew that kind of sorrow. "How many hired servants of my father have bread enough and to spare, and I perish with hunger?" It was that hunger and loneliness that started him on the homeward way. If he had never seen anything more in his trouble than that, he would never have been changed. He would still have been a prodigal in his father's house. A good meal and a soft bed would have comforted his heart, but it would have left him unsaved and harder than before. His would have been "the sorrow of the world that worketh death." But he listened to the deeper voice and it wrought repentance. He saw himself in the light of the father's love and was convicted of sin. He did with his sorrow what we all ought to do. He let it lead him to God. Out of the depth of his pain he said, "I will arise and go to my father." That is the way of healing.

XLII

THE CURE OF FUTILITY

"And Simon answering said unto him, Master, we have toiled all the night and have taken nothing: nevertheless at thy word I will let down the net."
LUKE 5: 5

CHRIST had come on these men at a bad moment. They had just returned from a night of fruitless fishing. He might have sympathized with them, as we would have done. But he was always full of surprises. Instead, he bade them launch out into the deep. In other words, he bade them go out at once and try again.

One of the commonest moods in life is that of futility. Most people feel it at some time or another. Many people feel it all the time. In his last novel Mr. Priestley shows it up in the modern world in nearly every page. He describes modern London—eight millions of people eating, drinking, sleeping. "And what it is all about nobody knows," he says. "Eight millions rolling on in one vast mystery." A question from the prophet Isaiah whispers itself in thousands of hearts. "Wherefore do ye spend money for that which is not bread, and your labor for that which satisfieth not?"

216

But Christ has an answer for that mood. His answer is practical. "Launch out into the deep," he said to Peter and the rest. It meant going back to their work again, but his words have a meaning below the surface of them. They suggest the reason of most of our futility. We have not been living for anything big enough or deep enough to satisfy our hearts. There is that in all of us that will not be content with merely doing little things— adding up figures, cooking, and washing, even running a factory or buying and selling a multitude of things. There must be something more in life than that. God has something very big on hand in which He wants us to share. He is seeking to change men and women. He wants to fill the world with love instead of hatred, to build bridges of fellowship, to bring in his Kingdom. That purpose we can share just where we are. The old story of the three men at work on a cathedral will illustrate the point. Each was asked what he was doing. One said, "I am cutting a stone." The second said, "I am earning my wages." The third said, "I am helping to build a cathedral." He saw the building rising to the glory of God, and the thousands in days to come who would find Him there. He saw, in fact, behind his lowly work the coming Kingdom of God. He had launched out into the deep.

We of the Church also need a message like this. We, too, are sometimes invaded by the sense of

217

futility. We have moments when we feel that we have toiled and caught nothing. Is not our need just to launch out into the deep? There is a real danger of being content with our various activities. We have this and that meaning and service. The evenings are filled up with a multitude of doings. But is anything vital really happening? It is true we cannot measure spiritual results. These belong to God. But we must not let that sound truth become an excuse for shallow service. The Church's task is "to do business in great waters." It is not merely to keep people decent or make them a little better. It is to bring about a revolution in their hearts. Are we seeking for that? It is also to be the means of setting up God's rule on a world-scale. Are we trying for that? That is one reason why the work of missions overseas is vital to the life of the Church. Nothing less than God's purpose can satisfy our hearts.

It may be that we need to seek the deeper rule of Christ in our own lives. The other day a newspaper described what has recently happened to a farmer in South Africa. He had worked a small farm for thirty years, and had made little of it. One day he dug a little deeper in his plowing, and discovered that underneath the shallow soil, in which all his work had been done, was a stratum of gold-bearing quartz. When the rock was exposed he found a reward that put all his former earnings in

218

the shade. It is a little parable of many lives. We spend our toil on the surface and get little. But under the surface, in a deeper fellowship with Christ, there is treasure that would fill our lives with joy and power.

It may be that our sense of futility is mainly due to weariness and the failure which will sometimes meet us. We get tired and disheartened. We let our failures fill the view and hide the encouragements. Christ has a message for us here. It is to go back to the place where we have failed. But it is to go back with him and at his command. That makes a mighty difference. It takes the management of our work and our life from our own shoulders. It sends us out with the thrill of his voice in our souls and the assurance of his presence. A company of soldiers sent out on a task may get into a difficult place. They may get lost in the dust and conflict, and their courage ebbs away. But if at the moment their trusted captain appears, the whole position is changed. He knows the objective. He knows the way to it. He takes command. He brings the reinforcement of his own spirit. That is what happens when we face life with Christ in command. Our temptation is to lose sight of him. We become entangled in our difficulties, our failures, and our fears. Our need is to get him back at the center and take our orders from him.

These orders will sometimes be surprising. They may even contradict all our reasoning. He may take us into new paths of adventure. He may bid us tackle what we thought was the impossible. But the results will be surprising. Our doubts and our fears will be confounded. Like Peter, we shall feel that we are not worthy of so great a Master. For that was the real meaning of his self-reproachful cry. In very shame of his doubts and hesitations he fell on his knees and said, "Depart from me; for I am a sinful man, O Lord." It is indeed true, as has been said, that Christ is too big for our small hearts. But, if we trust him in utter obedience, he will make us equal to what he asks.

XLIII

DOING THINGS WE DISLIKE

*"If any man will come after
me, let him deny himself."*
MATT. 16: 24

THE word "self-denial" is a most unpopular word
today. It sounds narrow and old-fashioned. It
looks like shutting the door against life. We prefer
to talk in these days of "self-expression." We are
urged to be ourselves, to live out all that is in us,
to let ourselves go. Do not all things in nature live
by expressing themselves—the flowers in the garden, the birds in the trees? Why should it be otherwise with us? Christ himself said that he came that
we might find life, and might have it to the full.

But it was He also that said that we must deny
ourselves if we would follow him. He was very
direct and explicit about it. "If any man will come
after me, let him deny himself." The simplest way
to put it is to say that if we become his disciples we
must be prepared to do many things we dislike.
We will have to give up pleasure for duty. We will
have to give up our own way to take his way. He
will ask us to carry burdens which conflict with our

own inclinations. The way of love to others will mean the sacrifice of time and strength which we would rather spend in other ways. In St. Paul's words, we must "crucify the flesh and its affections and lusts." That means doing a good many things we do not like. Of course, it is not only Christ who asks this. If we would succeed in business, music, making a home, we will need to deny ourselves. The road to efficiency in any line of life is guarded by a narrow gate. The cost of attainment is always sacrifice. For efficiency means concentration. If we would use the sun's rays to kindle a flame, they must be focused in what is called a "burning glass." But that means that some of the rays which are otherwise diffused must be brought to a central point. So it is with life. If we would make a success of any effort, the rays of our diffused energy must be withdrawn and gathered into a point of purpose. It is well to face the fact and be prepared to discipline ourselves. Christ will ask us to do many things we do not like and to cease from some things we do like. It is this truth which the season of Lent brings before us. By an old custom of the Christian Church we are bidden, for a period, to practice some deliberate self-denial. We are reminded of the need of doing things we do not like.

But this self-denial is not an end in itself. Doing without things we like, and doing things we do not like both have a purpose. It is to help us to find life. It is to set us free from the tyranny of self. We are constantly tempted to follow our own desires, to do or enjoy only the things that we like. We tend to read the books we like, to eat things we like, to choose the friends we like. One result of this habit is that we become slaves of our own desires. The love of pleasure and ease gets hold of us. Our body may become pampered and refuse to obey the call of the spirit. When we are asked to do a bit of service or to take on some burden, our selfish desires stand in the way. We make excuses of one kind and another. But the real reason is that we have got into the habit of doing only what we like. We are bound with a chain. If we are to be free, the mean, proud, pampered self must be denied. We must bring the body into control if it is to be our servant and not our master. We must break the chain of selfish desire if we are to be free. This freedom is won by deliberately doing things we de not like. "I make it a habit," said a great teacher, "to deny myself in something every day just to keep my will in training." This discipline of the will is needed if we are to be the servant of Christ.

But self-denial is the gateway of life in another sense. Those who make a habit of doing only the things they like find themselves, before long, in a kind of prison. The things they like doing become fewer and fewer. For all the best things in life demand some trouble to get them or enjoy them. Learning music, for instance, is never easy. The power to enjoy the best books means concentration and perseverance. The making of friends means taking trouble to be kind and thoughtful. If we only do what we like, we shall find that bit by bit we shut ourselves out of the best things in life. Our dislikes will put up fences round us; before long these fences of dislike or prejudice will shut us into a very narrow world. If we are to find life to the full, we must break them down. We must do things we do not like. That is the only way to get out of our prison. It may mean mixing with people we do not care about, or cultivating friendships among those who are not of our class. It may be we must set ourselves to read some book we dislike. But the way out of narrowness into life is by the breaking down of some fence of prejudice or dislike.

This is most true of fellowship with Christ. He will ask us to help people we do not like, to get rid of reserve, to take trouble with unattractive people. When we do this, however hard, we shall find that we have opened a road into a new world of interest and affection. We shall find new capacities awakening in ourselves that were dying for lack of use. It is the same with reading the Bible, with prayer or worship. A psychologist in America has just written a book called *The Return to Religion*. He discovered in his work that religion is indispensable. But unbelief, pride, and prejudice had put up fences which had to be broken down. The first thing he did was to go back to church. His reason for going back was that it was one of the things he did not like. On the other side of that dislike was a rich country of experience from which, by this fence, he had been shutting himself out. We may not like reading the Bible to begin with. The habit of prayer may take a good deal of trouble to acquire. But on the other side of the fence of our dislike lies the fellowship of Christ. When he bids us do something we do not like, he is not seeking to narrow our life, he is showing us how to expand it. He is not stealing our joy. He is offering us freedom. He is bidding us break down a fence which has been keeping us out of life. He is asking us to dethrone self, that his love may come in to possess us and set us free.

THE WORDS FROM THE CROSS

XLIV

(1) FORGIVENESS

*"Father, forgive them; for
they know not what they do."*
LUKE 23: 34

THE way of the Cross for Jesus was in every step
of it a victory. The words he spoke in the midst
of his agony reveal it in every syllable. Every one
of them was significant. His infinite faith and love
break through in words that live through the ages.
It is good that in the days before Easter we should
study his mind as it is here disclosed. And this
first word from the Cross is the keynote of his
Spirit. It was this that converted the dying thief by
his side. It was this, also, which melted the hard
heart of the Japanese criminal, named by one who
wrote of him, "A Gentleman in Prison." "When
I read these words," he said, "I felt my heart
pierced as by a five-inch nail." A love that could
pray for the people who were doing him to death
could be no other than Divine.

The thing that strikes us first is His infinite charity. "They know not what they do." Few of us
are ready to think in this way of those who do us
ill. We do not imagine that they are ignorant or

229

forgetful. We remember all that we did for them. We recall our friendship, the kindly things we did, the favors we showed them. And all this heightens our indignation and sorrow. We imagine they must have been conscious of it all. Their act could be nothing less than base betrayal. So we think. We do not realize that passion and selfishness can blind the eyes. They were probably swept off their feet or overmastered by some sudden impulse that even in the act made them ashamed. Jesus knew that these enemies of his were blind. They did not know that they were crucifying the Son of God. They never dreamed that they were opposing God's will of tenderest love seeking them in Christ that he might save them. They did not know. Christ saw them through the eyes of his own perfect charity. Even of his enemies he said the best that could be said when they were making it agony for him to speak at all.

But this was not an excuse, and we must not be ready to take it so. It would be easy to apply that to our sins and tell ourselves that God will pardon because we did not know. But to take sin like that is to blind ourselves with a word that was meant to give us light. For this is a revelation of the real nature of all sin. It is always worse than we realize. These people were doing evil, but no worse than ours. For there are no degrees in sin; it is the same in its nature wherever we find it. They did not know that he was the Son of God. They thought he was just a peasant, an unknown man whose life did not matter. He was an inconvenience to them. He threatened their comfortable ways. To put him to death seemed a trifle. They did not know. But the real act of sin was just the callousness, the selfish cruelty, the lack of love and of honesty with truth. It is this spirit which is sin, and the sin is the same whoever we may sin against. We know not what we do when we are unkind whoever it may be that we hurt. It may be a little child or some casual stranger for whom no one cares. The unloving and callous spirit in any of us is of the same nature as that which crucified Jesus. This is what the Cross makes clear. Sin is that which thwarts and opposes the loving will of God and it still puts Him on a Cross.

The results of sin are the same even though we do not see them. Sin works out in unhappy homes, in slums, in misery and war. The root of all that mars the world is the evil we carry in our hearts. That is a fact and Calvary shows it up. The full results may be hidden from us, but they are there. If only we could see the results of sin it would make us hold our hand. That is the fact that comes home to us when we have sinned and the deed is done. If only we had known we would not have done it. If only we had seen what our temper or selfishness would do in the wrecking of home or the breaking

231

of the hearts of those we love. But we do not see till it is too late. Christ died to open our eyes. That broken body of Christ with the nails in his hands and feet is a symbol of the fruit of the evil that we all do. It is the bitter harvest of "our weak self-love and guilty pride." Christ was looking into all the misery and pain of the world when he said, "They know not what they do." He bore it in his own body that we might see it, and turn from it in penitence and shame.

It is when we see what sin is that we are ready to listen to His prayer for forgiveness. That cry of forgiveness was not his alone. It was not merely his plea to God. It was God's love breaking forth in him. It was not a cry of despair. It was a triumphant cry of love. There is nothing more victorious in all history. His love had triumphed over all the agony. Nothing could drown it or destroy it. It remained "constant through the watches long." Sin could not put out the light of it. That is a fact to which we can cling when the sense of sin overwhelms us. Our sin cannot keep him from loving us. Even when sin has done its worst, He loves on. He waits to take us back into his fellowship. There is no depth of evil, no shadow of betrayal, no pit of shame from which his love can be excluded. He stands by.

But there is even more. It was for this He died. He has won the right to offer us this forgiveness.

The Cross was something more than the revelation of sin in its true nature. It was even more than the revelation of triumphant love. It was an act of God Himself going forth in Christ to break the power of sin. Christ was claiming for us from God, in this prayer, the full fruits of his victory, which is our redemption. He never prayed for anything that he did not think was possible. And here he is asking for that which his death had made a reality. He is asking for the power to enable us to overcome. As we listen to him there we can be sure of forgiveness. For we can be sure that his prayer is answered. The one thing we have to do is to see what sin means and to take his fellowship freely and fully. What he asks for us is ours, for he has won it. All we need is with gratitude and love to take it in and to make it ours.

XLV

(2) SALVATION

*"Today thou shalt be
with me in Paradise."*
LUKE 23: 43

CHRIST had not long to wait for the first fruits of
his Cross. It would have been almost natural if
pain had given the dying thief no eyes for anyone
but himself. But even he saw Christ there. He
heard the prayer that came from his lips. He felt
the love that lay behind it, and it changed him
through and through.

He saw the reality of his own sin. What it had
been we do not know. It may have been some crime
against society. Or it may have been things that
society does not call sins. One of the first things
that happens when we see Christ truly is that things
we did not realize were sins come home to our conscience. They stand out. There are sins against love
in ordinary life that are worse than some of the
things which society condemns. We do not see
them till Christ's love shines in. Then we know
them for what they are. The landscape of the
moral world appears in its true perspective when
His light rises on it. The Cross brought convic-

tion of sin. "I saw how much God cared, and then I saw how little I cared." So wrote one whom Calvary had brought to God. So it was with the thief by the side of Jesus.

Conviction brought also confession. It is one thing to feel guilt. It is another thing to own it. That takes a good deal of honesty. It means the humbling of our pride. This man confessed his guilt to Christ. He also confessed it to his fellow-criminal. It was utter humiliation. For it was a point of pride with many a criminal to keep his head high to the last. But it meant the determination to live in the new world of moral realities. He was determined to be sincere. He was ready to be known for what he was—one who had been a thief, but was now honest with himself and with God. That was the first step to peace. He had no longer the need to keep up appearances even to himself. The light of Christ is the light of reality. Only when we are real with him and others can we have peace. But the confession of sin has power also in the very act of it. It brings the sense of release from sin. When we have humbled our pride to face sin in its reality and confess it, in a strange way it begins by that act to lose its power. It belongs to a past on which we have turned our back. And, like Christian in *Pilgrim's Progress,* we are on the way to the sepulcher where the love of Christ will loose our burden completely from us, and bury it out of sight.

But this man had also come into the vision of Christ as Lord. He had seen on the Cross no broken figure of defeat, but a Victor, a King. "Remember me," he prayed, "when thou comest into thy kingdom." That was marvelous insight. He had seen what the whole world had missed, the triumph of love, the victory over evil which made Calvary a throne. He had seen the glory of the Son of God. It was not so hard to call Christ Lord when he came forth in the splendor of his resurrection. But to see him as Lord when he was being shamefully done was a miracle of insight. And Christ had wrought it from his Cross. The gates of the Kingdom opened to this man there, and he looked and longed to be within. Christ's victory in him was complete. Guilty, lost, and helpless, as he knew himself to be, he had come to the point where he was ready for Christ to receive him and lead him in. There is no other way of entrance. We cannot enter the Kingdom of God with our head unbowed and all the banners of our pride unfurled. We can only enter it when it seems as if forever we must stand outside, and find the gates forever barred. Then and then only are they open to take us in.

It only remained for Christ to speak the word of welcome. And royally the word was spoken. "To-day thou shalt be with me in paradise." The word reveals Christ's perfect assurance in the heaven that waited for his coming. He had never really left it. For the spiritual world had been his home. The love of God had wrapped him round, it was the very air he breathed. The fellowship with the Father had been his all through. And neither pain nor evil could break it for a moment.

It was this world into which He welcomed the penitent. What the word "paradise" conveyed to him we can only imagine. It meant the fullness of Christ's fellowship. "With me" was the word of Christ. The very memory of sin was banished by that word. Its power would be utterly broken. No shadow from the past would darken the light. No hint of his crime would stray into the Father's welcome to his son, come home. If he remembered it himself, it would only fan the flame of gratitude and wonder. A new life was beginning for him in which he would have power to live in that new world to which Christ had opened his eyes. We can only ponder the wealth of that welcome and that assurance. It takes our breath away. Christ said very little about heaven in his teaching. But how near and how real it was his words on the Cross reveal. Not only sin will be gone. Pain also will be gone. All the weight of ills with which earth can sometimes load us will be lifted. Pain has its meaning and its message now. But there it will be over, for its work will be done. That also must have

237

filled the heart of this penitent sufferer with peace. What heaven is, in all its wonder, we cannot know. "Eye hath not seen, nor ear heard, the things which God hath prepared." As we come to Christ and let him speak to us, and his love penetrates our hearts, hopes awaken and kindle imagination. These hopes will all be fulfilled, for we shall be fully in his presence.

> How know I that blessedness befalls,
>   who dwell in Paradise,
> The outwearied hearts refreshing,
>   rekindling the worn-out eyes?
> Nay! much more than this I know,
>   for this is so:
>   Christ is there.

XLVI

(3) COMFORT

*"Woman, behold thy son!
. . . Behold thy mother!"*
John 19: 26, 27

We do not always realize what the Cross must have
meant for the mother of Jesus. No pain that it
brought to any of his friends could have been so
sore as that which it brought to her. She had nursed
him and cared for him up to manhood. She had
watched with growing fear the storm gathering
around his head, while she could only stand helplessly by. He had passed completely out of her
control into a world where she could not follow
him. And now at last he hung on a criminal's cross.
It was the last drop in a cup which grew ever more
bitter. All the time she had grown more lonely
and bereft. And now death was ending his life, and
leaving her a solitary stricken figure in a tragic
world.

But Christ was thinking of her. Even on the
Cross, where pain must have been so excruciating
as to absorb the mind, his first thoughts were of
others. It was the high-water mark of his selfless-
ness. First, he thought of his enemies, then of the

dying thief, and now also of his mother. His sensitiveness to the needs of men was keen as ever. There is comfort for us in all this. Though we forget him, he does not forget us. Even amid the pain we give him through our heedless selfish ways, his thought is for our needs. And among them is our need of comfort when death strikes home to our hearts with loneliness and sorrow. He has a word to say to us if we will listen. He had a heart of tenderness and love for those who are only conscious of the pang of an unhealed wound.

What could his words mean to Mary? "Woman, behold thy son!" Her son was dying. It must have seemed to her that no one could ever take his place. She had other sons, but they could never be to her what he had been. She had poured out on him her special affection. He filled a place in her heart that no other could take. Now this maternal affection was being frustrated, and the object of it snatched from her care. A good many people have passed through this experience. We are apt to feel, when the parting comes, that nothing can ever make up for the loss. So long as we cling to that idea, it is apt to make us unfit for the tasks of love in which God can use us still. There are others who need the love which we may waste in useless repining. A good many people fail just here when some big sorrow comes. They become absorbed in their grief. Their hearts close up around their pain, nursing it, even finding a comfort in the very sadness of it, till it becomes a kind of selfish luxury. They become enslaved to self-pity and shut up in their grief as in a prison. The only way out of this disabling sorrow lies in helping and comforting others who are waiting for our care. Many a broken life has blossomed again into joy through seeking to blossom for others. It may be a child has been taken and they are sorely wounded. But they do not let grief close their hearts; they rather let it open them to others who need comfort. Instead of letting sorrow blind their eyes, their very tears enable them to see more clearly the griefs of others. Their own suffering makes them more sensitive. It gives them a new experience through which they have power to heal and comfort. Others will listen to us just because we have suffered and found victory. The comfort we have received of God becomes a ministry to others. So, through the sad experience, new doors of service and usefulness are opened, till in the end we find that the very sorrow which made us lonely makes us a center of vital friendships. So Jesus bade his mother take her eyes from himself and her loss of him, and fix them on another who in his pain needed the comfort she could give.

His word to John was the same. "Behold thy mother!" She needed a son's love, and all the more because she was growing old and probably feeble.

241

It is not easy for young people with their troubles to remember those who are growing aged. "Remember the gray birds," an old lady used to say to young people in a whimsical way. She was thinking of those who are not so interesting to the young, because they are growing old and lonely and depressed with the sorrows of life. The young have their own vital interests, and the griefs of ageing people are apt to make them unattractive. So Jesus bade John take Mary into his care and think of her as a mother. There can be no more beautiful ministry than to be tender and reverent with those whom the years have left stranded and alone.

The words "mother" and "son" on the lips of Jesus were not merely figures of speech. It was part of his teaching that his love breaks all barriers. It creates a spiritual relationship which is even deeper and more real than that of blood or family. "He that doeth the will of God," he once said, "is my brother, and my sister, and mother." In his world of love, the family circle widens and includes all who are one with him. His fellowship creates a bond that makes us brethren. When we come into the family of God through him, there is a union that is closer than blood-brotherhood. The household of faith is the finest product of human relationships. Comforting one another and sharing our love for him, we find a fellowship in which the wounds of sorrow are healed. We are brought into a world

which is eternal. John and Mary went home together as Christ had bidden them, comforting each
other for his sake. But they found, as we know
when we turn the page and read of the Resurrection, that he was with them in a new way. The
Cross had not taken him from them. It had made
Him more fully theirs. They had come into a fellowship in which sorrow is overcome. They had
entered through his love into a world in which there
is no more death.

XLVII

(4) LONELINESS

*"My God, my God, why
hast thou forsaken me?"*
MATT. 27 : 46

IN this cry from the depths, the pit of our Lord's
agony opens up its darkness. We can see but a
little way into it, for none of us has his sensitiveness of spirit, or his quality of love. The agony
was of the spirit more than of the body. The
physical side of it must have been beyond our imagination. But his pain went deeper. "We suffer
alone; we die alone," says Amiel. "The heart knoweth its own bitterness." That was most true of all
for Christ.

This pain was a twofold experience. It was "the
double agony in Man for man." It was the pain of
a heart that realized the awfulness of human sin—
the mockery of goodness, the refusal to love at its
best, the utter rejection of God. But there was
something more. For Christ was one with human-
ity, and he felt to his very soul the shame and dishonor of this crime they were committing. We ourselves can understand this in part. We can suffer
in the evil that is done to ourselves. But along with

244

that we can also feel the shame that those who are our brothers can fall so low. A father bears this twofold weight of sin in the deeds of a son gone wrong. He suffers in the wrong done to himself. He may have his son's debts to pay. He may have to work hard just when he should be resting to carry a burden that his boy's extravagance and folly have thrown upon him. But he also suffers in the fact that one to whom he is bound by ties of blood and affection has been so guilty. No word of Christ gives us deeper insight into the quality of his love for us than this cry from the depths.

But this pain brought the sense that God had forsaken him. The tempest of evil had driven him into a world from which it seemed as if God were shut out. It was as if God had left the universe to take its own way to destruction, and Christ was at the mercy of the evil uncontrolled. The sense of God's presence was lost. Moments like that may come to us all in lesser degree. We may feel this sense of dereliction when, for instance. we see the world letting itself be driven into a race of armaments. Or it may come when sorrow and misfortune pile themselves one after another on our heads. It looks then as if the world were empty of God. We are only conscious of evil. Like the Ancient Mariner we feel ourselves alone, so lonely "that God himself scarce seemed there to be."

We may well ask, however, if the very fact that

we feel so deeply the pain and sin of the world does not really mean the nearness of God. "If I make my bed in hell, thou art there," wrote the Psalmist. Our very sense of evil means that God is there. It is He who creates this capacity to feel. The Father was never nearer to our Lord than when he so deeply bore the world's sin that he felt him to be absent. It is a comfort to feel that Christ knows these dark depths. He had his hours when the clouds hid the sun. He knew the darkness in which the very stars are gone. And there, if we stretch out our hand, we can feel the grasp of his, and it will hold us firm. There is no door of loneliness and pain through which he has not gone before us. The place of despair can never be utterly desperate since he has been there.

But even in this dark and lonely hour Christ had his consolations. The words of his cry were part of the 22d Psalm. We are justified in thinking that he was repeating it to himself, finding comfort in it. If we read it, we may get some idea of the background of his mind in this hour when God's presence was hidden. Was he not falling back for comfort on one or two things which we also may rest upon when the black night of doubt comes down?

There was, for one thing, the knowledge that He had been called of God. From his very birth he had known God's love. This was a fact he could never forget. It was the central experience of his life. We, too, in our dark hours can fall back on past experiences of God. That is part of their value. There are things we cannot forget. We can think of moments when we knew that God had surely guided. There have been hours and days when the clearest voice in our souls was the challenge of God. These experiences refuse to be dissolved away by any mist of doubt. Memory as well as hope can be the anchor of the soul when the storm is up and the tempests drive.

There are also the experiences of others. "Our fathers trusted in Thee and were not confounded." That also strengthened the soul of Jesus, and it may strengthen ours. Our own convictions may fade. Doubts may overtake us. But behind our own faith lie the victories of God's love in the souls of countless others. These are the most certain facts in history. We are not on this road alone. We belong to a great succession of those who have fought a good fight and have kept the faith. When the light fails in our hearts for the moment, we can look back and see it shining clear and strong along the road that troubled souls have traveled in the sure company of God.

But the Psalm ends in triumph. A mighty hope rings through the closing words. Into that hope, the stricken hearts of those who have held on have always come triumphantly. "The kingdom is the

Lord's, and he is the governor among the nations. All the ends of the earth shall remember and turn unto the Lord." Through the darkness there shone in the soul of Christ this light of final victory. The assurance of God's reign returned, and evil lost its paralyzing power. This also we may take for our comfort. It will help us to hold on. The dark hour will pass for us as it passed for him, if in his strength we endure.

> No cloud across the sky but passes at the last
> And gives us back the face of God once more.

"Weeping may endure for a night, but joy cometh in the morning." All the saints have found it so. So it was for Christ. And so shall it be for us.

XLVIII

(5) LONGING

"Jesus said, I thirst."
JOHN 19: 28

EACH of the seven words Christ spoke on the Cross
is a window into his soul. Even this simple cry of
physical need has more in it than appears on the
surface. It is a comfort to us to realize that he
passed through the ordeal of physical pain. It
is a link that binds us to him. The sick and
weary sufferer with pain-parched lips can at
least know that Christ himself knew that experience. Pain is a very absorbing thing. It shuts
us up to the grim fact. It makes everything else
of no account. We cannot even think. Sometimes not even pray. Thought is for calm hours of
reflection. But at least we can remember him at
that moment, and in that memory of his pain and
weariness there is a link of fellowship. We are one
with him there. He suffered to make us feel this
bond. That link with Christ which is forged in
pain is the assurance that our pain has meaning.
In that assurance there is peace. With that, we can
wait the hour of illumination. That word of his,

"I thirst," is like a hand held out, and in its grasp there is strength to endure.

But when we look deeper, this word of his has more to say. It revealed, for instance, his quiet acceptance of his Cross. You or I might have been tempted to keep from showing our suffering. We hate to expose our weakness before our enemies. We should not want to give them the satisfaction of seeing how much we were suffering. Christ thought nothing of this. He would not shirk one pang. He had chosen to walk that road. If they jeered at his suffering, so it must be. It was part of his humiliation.

> His are the thousand sparkling rills
> That from a thousand fountains burst,
> And fill with music all the hills;
> And yet He saith, "I thirst."

Nor did he refuse the help they offered him. We might have been tempted to reject their service. It would have hurt our pride to receive it. We could not have taken it from the hands that had wounded us so. But there was no resentment in Christ's heart. There was no barrier to friendship even with his murderers. Nothing reveals his freedom from every bitter or angry feeling more than his acceptance of the little service that they did for him, when at last they had made him their prey. For the hardest thing we can do is to accept some gift or service from people who have hurt us or done us ill.

It is harder even than to do them some service. The latter may be done without loss of the dignity which is akin to pride. But to be in need and to take help from those who have brought us there is the last humiliation. It is the very dregs of the cup of bitterness. To take it as he took it is the victory of love. Jesus accepted his weakness and wore it for a crown. It was love in all the beauty of perfect self-forgetfulness.

But surely these words speak of a deeper longing. In his heart there burned an unquenchable thirst for the souls of men. His whole life had been spent in seeking. The picture he drew of the shepherd on the hills tracking down the one sheep that was lost was his picture of his own life. It was he who went out on that journey risking everything, shirking no pain or weariness or danger and never giving up, however hopeless the search. There was nothing selfish in that love. He wanted nothing for himself. His only passion was to bring men to themselves by restoring them to the love of God. It was of them that he thought all the time, never of his own satisfaction. He did not seek to be loved for anything that love would bring to him, but only for what it would bring to those he loved. For he knew that for men to love himself was to love goodness and purity and unselfishness. And that is to be saved.

Our love is often a very different thing. We seek

to be loved, not realizing that that longing is a selfish thing and will bring no real satisfaction. We seek to possess the affection of others, not knowing that there is a higher thing than being loved. That better thing is to love whether the love be returned or no. That alone satisfies and ennobles. Among other things, it is that power to love other people of which he spoke when he said, "He that drinketh of the water that I shall give him shall never thirst; but the water that I shall give him shall be in him a well of water springing up into eternal life." That love for others is the thirst which is always its own satisfaction. This thirst possessed him and at the same time was the secret of his joy. It is this love into which he seeks to win us. When we come to know it and our love goes out to others for the mere sake of what we can help them to be, we have been won by him. We have been saved into his likeness.

But it can only happen as we see his love for us. And how better can we realize it then when we hear him say, "I thirst"?

> But more than pains that racked Him then
>   Was the deep longing thirst Divine
> That thirsted for the souls of men;
>   Dear Lord! and one was mine.

In one of his sermons D. L. Moody, the great evangelist, drew a picture of this unconquerable love. "I can imagine that when Christ said to the little band around him, 'Go ye into all the world and preach the gospel, beginning at Jerusalem,' Peter said in reply, 'Lord, do you really mean that we should go back to Jerusalem and preach the gospel to those men who murdered you?' 'Yes,' said Christ. 'Go, hunt up that man that spat in my face. Tell him that he may have a seat in my Kingdom yet. Yes, Peter, go, find the man that made that cruel crown of thorns and placed it on my brow, and tell him I will have a crown ready for him when he comes into my Kingdom, and there will be no thorns in it. Search for the man that drove the spear into my side and tell him there is a nearer way to my heart than that.'" That is the love that comes out to seek us from the Cross. Can any of us resist it? Can any of us fail to see that it is for us he came? There is a place in that love that is all our own.

XLIX

(6) ACCOMPLISHMENT

"It is finished."
JOHN 19: 30

THESE words are often used by us when we have
brought something to a close. They mark the end
of a long pain or a big strain, and sometimes the
end of life itself. But in no case have they had
such meaning as they had on the lips of our Lord.
They marked the end of his agony. There are
some experiences which we cannot help being grateful to be done with. However much they may
have to give us, it is a relief to have them over.
There was this relief in the mind of Christ. But
not relief only. There was also the comfort of
knowing that the hour of physical agony had not
been stained by any consciousness of defeat. He
had not slipped even for a moment into any mood
of complaint or bitterness. The battle was over
and he had not lost one bout with the tempter.

It marked, of course, also, the end of his life.
He was at the most only thirty-seven. In other
cases there is both pathos and tragedy in a life of
such usefulness and promise thus cut short. Milton
laments the tragic end of his friend Lycidas, "dead

ere his prime." Death was "the blind fury with the abhorred shears who slits the thin-spun life." But there was no sense of tragedy and defeat in the soul of Jesus as he thought of the end. His life was finished in the true sense of the word. None of it was unfulfilled. He had no sense of frustration. "So little done; so much to do," said Cecil Rhodes as he lay dying. That is the feeling that all have, however full life may have been. But our Lord's life was complete. He had followed perfectly the will of God. Every duty had been done. Every task small or great had been completed. His life had been one long steady fulfilment of God's purpose as it met him day by day. There were no loose ends in the finished web. It was, all through, a perfect response to the call of God. Even at thirty-seven it was a finished life. And his heart was full of peace.

But the words had an even deeper significance. For he had come to do the one thing, and that was done. He had come to show the world what God is really like. In him God had acted. And the Cross was the end of that act of God. There God's purpose of love came to its crown. That purpose dominated Christ's life all through, from first to last. "I have a baptism to be baptized with," he once said, "and how am I straitened till it be accomplished?" It is impossible to put into words what he put into the Cross. But this at least we can say: He won a victory there which through the Cross he offers to us. It was the victory of God's love over human sin and lovelessness. Something was done by God at Calvary which does not need to be done again. The gate of new life was opened for us all. No more need we lie helpless under the weight of sin and fear. No more need we doubt God's perfect love.

> He only could unlock the gate
> Of heaven and let us in.

And on the Cross the gates were unlocked. The prison door was flung open, and we are free to walk out into the light of God's love and the completeness of his fellowship. It was this accomplishment that was in Christ's mind when he said, "It is finished."

These words of Christ bring assurance and hope. God has done for us all that our salvation demands. Complete forgiveness is in these words. Some people find it hard to believe in forgiveness. It may be because we find it so hard to forgive others, or it may be because we find it so hard to forgive ourselves. Some lives are spoiled by the haunting sense of the sins and failures that lie in the past and throw their shadow over the future. We have repented of them. There is nothing we would not do to be done with them. But still they cling to us. For us this message comes with the assurance that has the Cross behind it. "Though they be red like crimson, they shall be white as snow."

There is also completeness of power for all the things God sets us to do as we seek to share His purpose and to be used of Him. That also Christ makes clear. That was why he could face the Cross and its apparent defeat with unconquerable hope. "Be of good cheer," he said; "I have overcome the world." And the echo of that triumph is in this word. He bids us take his victory and make it ours. Faith in Christ means all that.

In these words are focused Christ's light upon our life. The meaning of life is to share God's purpose. Each of us has a place in it. We are not here for nothing. There is something for which God is seeking to use us. To see that purpose of love and to give ourselves to be possessed and guided by it is the secret of life. Only as we give ourselves to that purpose is our life truly fulfilled. It matters not how long or successful life may appear on the surface. If we have served ourselves and our own ambitions, we have failed, and life lacks its true fulfilment. However short life may be, if that purpose has laid hold of us and we have given ourselves to it from day to day, life is complete. It is fulfilled in the measure in which we become the channels of that love. Our place may be a very limited one. We may spend our time on a sickbed. Our post of duty may be a humble home or a quiet

corner in some unknown village. That matters
nothing, if there we are seeking to know God's purpose and to be one with it. Some of the fullest lives
have been crippled by illness or limited by circumstances. They have been unknown to the world.
But they did the will of God. They were laid hold
of by His love and gave themselves up to what He
could do through them. And that is life at the full.
We have taken our place in His plan. And through
that obedience and loyalty our capacities are developed and brought to their best. Wherever life
may have been spent or whatever it may have
brought us, if we have followed Him we also may
end on this triumphant note and say, "It is finished."
We can be sure it will have found its place in God's
plan.

L

(7) TRUST

*"Father, into thy hands
I commend my spirit."*
LUKE 23: 46

CHRIST's name for God was Father. It was thus
He always spoke of Him and to Him, and he main-
tained it to the last. There is nothing more triumphant in the region of faith. He had known
God as Father through the placid years. In childhood he had always been "about his Father's business." The temple was his Father's house. The
world also was his Father's world. William Wat-
son speaks of the world as a house whose owner is
unknown.

> On from room to room I stray,
> Yet my host can ne'er espy.

For Jesus everything in the world spoke of the
Father. The lilies in the fields whispered of his
love. The birds sang of his care. But this was no
fair-weather faith. Through the thunder and the
tempest, amid the deepest agony that man has ever
suffered, he could still look up and say, "Father."
And with his last breath he sounds again the note

259

of perfect trust. "Father, into thy hands I commend my spirit."

This fact is one of the strongest arguments for our faith. It has been said that his faith in God's Fatherhood only holds in the sunshine. It is easy to believe it when the world is smiling. But can we believe it amid the cruelties of pain and evil? A mountain-climber describes how lovely the mountains look when his heart is high with courage. But when things are difficult and dangerous the face of the rocks becomes dark and menacing. Nature in herself has no steady comfort for us. Her face is but the mirror of our own moods. So it is with life. It changes its color for us with our own feelings. People often say that faith is like this. It comes and goes according to the changing weather. But Christ's faith had deeper foundations. His conviction of God's perfect love and care stood the test of Calvary. That is the strength of our conviction that God's love is real. If he had not suffered so, we might well have wondered if his Faith were not a fancy born of the sunshine. But on the Cross where he suffered every element of human pain, even to the betrayal of love, God's love was the strongest thing in his experience. That makes us sure of it. Only the truth could have held him fast through that experience. No phantasy could have carried him through it. The love of God was reaching him still amid the shadows of death. It was the most real thing in all his world. And it remained. When all was dissolving, there was rock beneath his feet. Underneath him were the Everlasting Arms, and he felt their grasp and sank back in peace. Surely the love that was so strong and enduring, when everything seemed to deny it, is a love on which we, too, can rest.

His last act was an act of perfect trust. Did he know precisely what lay beyond? Or was his view limited like ours? We sometimes think that the future life was all perfectly clear and certain to him. We think that death was no adventure into the unknown for Jesus. But did he know, by some knowledge not open to us, the secret of the many mansions? If that were so, would it not seem to make his faith somewhat less heroic than ours? For we cannot know the future in that precise way. We can only imagine it through the insight which sees what God's love implies. Our knowledge of the future comes only of our faith in God. So it was also for Jesus. That was part of his self-limitation. It was part of the human lot which he took on himself. And so when death came to him, it was enough for him that God took his Spirit into his care. He could leave all the rest in His hands.

That also must be enough for us. There is no scientific proof of a future life. Argument and reason will help us, but only when we have seen the love of God in Christ. Spiritualism may claim to

261

give us knowledge like what we have of things material. But it can tell us nothing of the things which God has prepared for those who love Him. Such knowledge belongs to another sphere. Only the insight which love awakens can make us sure of the things of the spirit. Love cannot be weighed or measured. And there are no mechanical devices by which we can look into the unseen world. It becomes real only to the heart which trusts.

To know that God is Father, because we have seen His love in Jesus, is to be sure that all that is best awaits us beyond. What uses God has for us there we do not know. What service He will appoint we cannot tell. What further education of our spirit lies before us we know not. In those hands of God there is infinite wisdom and skill. The wounds which earth has made will find their healing. The powers frustrated here will be released. "There shall be no more death, neither sorrow nor crying, neither shall there be any more pain." We think of those cut off in tender years from all earth might have given. Surely in that blessed country, they will find the reality of which earth's best is but a shadow. We do not know. But we know Him, and in that love which made us and sent Jesus to make Himself known there will be all we need. It is a great mystery, but it is a mystery of love. In that love we can rest and leave the future with our Father.

It is enough that He knows all,
And we shall be with Him.

This act of self-committal to God is the final step of faith. It will be ours, too, if like Jesus we have been meeting things all the way in that faith. It is now we must prepare for it, till faith becomes the habit of our life. Then, when the shadows gather and death clouds the mind, we can follow Christ in trust. That is all God needs to make it possible for Him to take us and give us His best. With this prayer we may leave the doubts that weakness brings, when the mind is no longer strong enough to withstand them. It is the final answer to all the menacing fears of heart and conscience. "Father, into thy hands I commend my spirit." The hand of death is powerless to take us out of the hands of God.

LI

ARE WE WITNESSES?

*"This Jesus hath God raised
up, whereof we are witnesses."*
Acts 2: 32

WE sometimes forget that the message of the Apostles was the good news of the Resurrection. That was the core of the first recorded sermon. It was preached by Peter, as we might imagine, and it converted thousands.

A scholar goes so far as to say that without the doctrine of the Resurrection, Christianity would die. This sounds a little startling. Would not the Sermon on the Mount remain? Of course it would, for it has a firm hold of our consciences. Would not the beauty of Christ's earthly life remain? Of course it would. Nothing can ever destroy that. Would not the belief in God remain? Of course it would. For our conviction of God's reality does not depend on the Resurrection. But none of these things are the Gospel.

When Christ rose from the dead, one or two things became crystal clear to the disciples and those to whom they told the story. One of these was that his way of life is victorious in the long run.

That was what they had doubted, and especially when he had been seized and crucified and buried. "That's over and done with," said his enemies. "We shall not have our consciences troubled any more." His friends were tempted to the same conclusion, though it brought them not relief but despair. They were tempted to think that his goodness was a kind of exotic. It did not belong to this world. It could not stand the crushing power of brute force. But when he rose, they knew that his kind of goodness is the very basis of the world. It is the only true way of life. It is a flower that can survive in the dreariest desert. It cannot be destroyed by the iciest wind.

But it meant also another great fact. It meant that God's power was at work victoriously. Christ had come speaking to them of God's purpose. He had shown them how God is at work fulfilling his will of love, bringing in his Kingdom. He had even told them that the Kingdom had come. He had assured them it was present in himself. It looked incredible. Then came Calvary and that dream seemed shattered. But when he rose from the dead, everything was changed. God was surely at work in Christ. Nothing that men could do could defeat him. Nothing could thwart his rule and bring his plans to dust. He had made even the wrath of men to praise him. He had taken the very Cross on which they had crucified His Son and made it the means

265

of his victory over death. What they had used to break his power had actually released it. "This Jesus hath God raised."

Can we wonder that thousands were converted by that message? It is just that which the world needs today; for it has lost heart and it has lost hope. Many have become cynical. Young people are afraid to look into the future. They can see nothing beyond, except the ghoulish victory of barbarous force. They tell us, too, that the Sermon on the Mount is lovely but impracticable. It will not work in modern business. It has no place in modern politics. Christ's day is done. He is being hurried again to his Crucifixion. This time it will be the end. So some think. So also they thought when he was crucified. So men have often thought through the long years since then. For at times faith has sunk so low that it seemed gone forever. But Christ lives. He triumphed; and in his living spirit is the assurance of the triumph of his way of life and the final victory of God's purpose. That is the confidence we need. That alone can bring hope back to the heart.

But how can we be sure of the Resurrection? The disciples gave one proof. They said they had seen it. "We are witnesses." That was conclusive; but not merely because they said it. There was something else that brought conviction. They had evidently had an experience that had changed them. A few weeks before, as many in the listening crowd well knew, they were broken men. They had lost hope. They were so frightened that they ran from the Cross and remained in hiding. They dared not lift their voices in the streets. But now there was a joy, a courage, a faith, a love, that made their faces shine. Their voices had a new ring. Something of their story had passed into their blood. They were like men who had the secret of victory over both sin and death. That was what brought conviction and made their witness credible. Their good news was reflected in their lives and in their spirit.

It is that witness the world needs today. It will begin to believe in the risen Christ when it sees him reflected in us, and in our victory over sin and fear and unbelief. That experience is possible. We also can say, "We are witnesses." We must find the power to say it. Nothing else will bring conviction. A friend of mine in the States was being examined for ordination. They asked him if he was converted. He said, "Certainly." They went on to ask, "How do you know?" Like a flash came the reply, "Because I was there!" It was a fact. He had been at a place where Christ met him and changed his life.

We ought to be able to say the same about the Resurrection. For it is not merely a physical fact taking place in a geographical locality. It is a spiritual experience. It happens within our souls.

> I envy not the Twelve.
> Nearer to me is He.
> The life that once He lived on earth
> He lives again in me.

An old negro spiritual recalls the main events in Christ's life, and asks the question, "Were you there?" "Were you there when they crucified my Lord?" "Were you there when he rose up from the grave?" The Christ who rose still lives. The Resurrection experience is a present and permanent possibility for each of us. The physical does not matter. The reality of the presence of a friend is shown by what passes from his mind and spirit into ours. The rest does not count. So we still may meet the risen Christ and know the victory of his Spirit.

The way to it is to let our minds expand to take the good news in. That is the first step. The next is to offer ourselves as completely to him as did the disciples. Then we shall know. But more than this. His victory will be reflected in our lives and our spirit. We shall be able to say, "We are witnesses," and when we say it, there will be that in us which gives our witness power.

LII

WHY PRAY?

*"Your heavenly Father knoweth what things
ye have need of, before ye ask him."*
                                    MATT. 6: 8

ONE of the things Jesus insisted on was that we
should pray. He himself prayed often and long.
He impressed on us God's willingness to give. "Ask,
and ye shall receive." If we who are sinful, and
whose lives are a patchwork of love and selfishness,
leap at the chance of helping our children, how much
more will God? God's heart burns with the passion
to give. He even knows what it is we need before
we ask Him. All this is a wonderful encouragement to pray. It should make the hour of prayer
the happiest hour of the day. For in that secret
room there is a welcome for us, when we go with
our troubles and needs, that should take away all
our hesitation and fear. We should have the same
feeling about God as we have about some rich and
generous friend, who makes us feel that he thinks
it a privilege to be asked for advice or help. If
we thought long enough of that picture of God, it
would make prayer as natural as breathing.

But this thought of God raises some questions in the mind about prayer. If God knows what we need before we ask Him, why tell Him? Why should we need to put our desires into words? There is this further question, also, that has troubled many people. If God is so ready to give, why should He wait for our prayers? Why should we need to pray at all? A mother does not wait for her little child's requests. He cannot always put them into words. He does not always know what he really wants or needs. But her love is ever watchful and she knows and supplies it. If we then know and supply our children's needs without their asking, why not God? Why should we need to ask?

There are, of course, a good many things that come to us without our asking for them. When we are born we come into a home prepared for us. All we need is ready to hand. Many, indeed, go through life in that condition. They hardly need to ask for anything. It is all supplied, so that they are scarcely conscious of any needs at all. They never know what it is to be in want of food. They have never had any difficulty in getting clothes or furniture, or any other thing. But this is not a healthy condition. A millionaire was walking with a friend along a city street, when they stopped to look into a window full of expensive jewels. "I would give much," said the rich man, "if I could see something that I

270

could not buy." If all our wants were supplied as if by magic, without any effort on our part, life would become very stale. It is the sense of need and the effort to satisfy it that gives to life most of its zest. The sense of need may be very painful, but it has inspired man's creative efforts and made possible his finest discoveries. Why did not God supply us with electric light all ready-made? Why did we have to learn the secrets of medicine by slow and painful groping? The reason must be that by the need and the effort to discover and invent, there are capacities of mind developed which could have been awakened no other way. God trains us through the needs that life awakens. Is it not the very sense of need which opens our minds to the existence of God Himself?

> "There is no God," the foolish saith,
>   But none, "There is no sorrow."
> And nature oft the cry of faith
>   In bitter need will borrow.

The consciousness of God comes to birth within us in a prayer of need which trouble or sorrow wrings from the heart.

Even though it be for nothing else than to bring us to God, it is good that we should need to pray. Otherwise we might never know Him. He might remain undiscovered, as electricity would have been had man been content with tallow candles. To have communion with God is the real fruit of prayer.

271

Even if none of our petitions were answered, it would be reward enough to have come into touch with Him. For our greatest need is God Himself. St. Augustine was right when he prayed, "Come, O Lord, in much mercy down into my soul, and take possession and dwell there. Give me Thine own self, without which, though Thou shouldst give me all that ever Thou hast made, yet could not my desires be satisfied." God's greatest gift is Himself. But we would not have found Him had not the sense of need brought us to seek Him.

There is something more to be said. Prayer would not have been our deepest impulse if God had not needed our prayers. The door by which God enters our life opens from our side, and prayer is the lifting of the latch. God needs our prayers to make it possible for Him to give us His best. There are things we cannot give others until they want them and feel the need of them. All parents know this by bitter experience. They can give their children food and clothing without their asking them. But the best things cannot be given to them till they want them. We cannot give our children advice if they do not want it. We cannot give them a real education until they desire it. There are secrets we long to tell them, and guiding we would like to give them. But if they do not feel the need of it and are not willing to learn, we are helpless. A famous violinist had a daughter who went to learn music from a stranger. Someone asked the father if he would not like to teach his daughter himself. "There is nothing I would like more," he said, "but I must wait till she asks me. There are things I cannot impart to her till she is ready for them and comes to ask for them."

Is it not the same with us and God? There are things He wants to give us. But He cannot impart them till we are ready to receive them. He cannot help us till we want His help, which means that we have discovered our helplessness. He cannot give us His Spirit till we have found out how unlike Christ we really are. He cannot draw us from the pit of selfishness or pride till we have become conscious of our plight, and in despair have stretched out a hand that He can grasp. For that moment He stands waiting with all the resources of His love.

273

LIII

THE DANGER OF ANSWERED PRAYER

"He gave them their request; but sent leanness into their soul."
Ps. 106: 15

SOME of us are much perplexed by the problem of unanswered prayer. But here is a case where prayer was answered, and the result was tragic. The Israelites were on their way through the desert. They had many hardships to face and enemies to fight. They had to meet with hunger and thirst and loneliness. It was all part of their training. But they resented it. They did not think of the possible blessedness of the rough road. They only felt the pangs of hunger and the sting of trouble. So they prayed that things might be made easier and that they might have a comfortable time. And God answered their prayer. They got what they wanted; but there was a heavy price to pay. For they lost the qualities that struggle would have brought into their life. They became blind to goodness and deaf to the voice of God. They became incapable of God's fellowship. The spiritual world was closed to them for lack of the power to live in it. It was the inevitable result of rejecting the discipline of life. God gave them their request, but sent leanness into their soul.

It is a warning to us to beware of the things we desire. For these are the things we really pray for, whatever our lips may say. That is a fact that should make us think. What do we really want? What is it in the depths of our hearts we are really seeking? That is our real prayer.

It is a terrifying fact that life often gives us what we really want. If we do not get it in form, we get it in substance. If we are seeking pleasure, our steps will lead us in roads that bring it. If we are ambitious, we will force a way to our desire. Laziness may keep success from us; but if we want anything and go out for it, we will probably get it. The tragic thing is that we will also get the kind of soul that goes along with it. Our desires will shape our character. We cannot seek comfort and pleasure and our own way as the chief things in life without spiritual poverty. That means the loss of love and faith, and the grace that comes through fellowship with God.

It is not good for us to get all we want. We see that very clearly in the case of children. No wise parent gives his child all he asks for. That way lies ruin. A rich man in the States took his boy to a well-known public school. He said to the schoolmaster, "I had a hard time in my youth. My boy is to have everything he wants. He can have as much money as he likes. All his whims are to be humored." To his surprise the schoolmaster replied, "I am sorry we cannot take your boy. He would ruin himself; and if he came here on those terms he would corrupt the school. You are trying to defraud your boy of the very discipline that has enabled you to succeed." The schoolmaster was right. The best training for children may be the discipline of learning to do without. For in that way they have a chance to learn what the real things are and to appreciate them.

It is as true of us as it is of a child. We may receive our requests and find leanness of soul. We may set our heart on things which may not be good for us to have. We may put the wrong things first. We may, for instance, set our heart on some ambition till it masters our will and directs our life. Stevenson says that a man can get £2,000 a year if he is willing to pay for it. He may put all his thought and energy into getting money. The result is that his better nature is starved. He gives up prayer; he ceases to find interest in worship. The spiritual world becomes unreal to him. He loses interest in the service of others. He is starving his better nature. He gets what he wants, but he loses his soul. The same thing may happen in the pursuit of comfort or reputation. We may be successful in life but failures in living. We may get our desires, and become in the process hard and proud and selfish. "The interests of the flesh," says Paul, "mean death; the interests of the spirit mean life and peace."

The same thing may happen in another way. We may seek something which in itself is good but is not the best. Conscience bids us take a stern way with ourselves. But we struggle against it. At length its protest is silenced. We cease to have scruples within. God has lifted His hand and let us go. We get what we want. But we have lost the rich treasure of His friendship. The higher level to which He would have led us is closed to us. Our inner life has lost its peace. Our influence has been robbed of its power. It is a tragic thing to seek our own way in defiance of what God asks of us. The way of self-pleasing may be strewn with roses, but it ends in trouble and tears.

There is a choice we must all make. It is that between God's way and our own. It is that between what Christ asks of us, and what we want for ourselves. Sometimes life refuses us what we want. It breaks our plans. It denies our request. The way we set for ourselves is barred by misfortune or failure. In that case we should thank God for the refusal, and seek to find His way. For whatever barriers life may set to our feet, the way of His will is always open. And often we find it by the refusals of life. Some of the most truly successful lives have found the key to real fulfilment through a failure at the beginning.

> I would have worked; God bade me rest.
> I would have gone; God bade me stay.
> He broke my will from day to day,
>   And said me "Nay."

That sometimes happens. If we look deeply we will find His guiding in the hand of failure or disappointment. Some of those who have influenced the world for good have found their call to service because the road of ambition which they had set for themselves was blocked by failure. Disappointment and failure have always a divine meaning if we will look for it. The question they bid us ask is what God is seeking to make us or to give us.

But if life gives us success, we must search and examine our real desires to find out if they are in the way of His will for us. Otherwise they are dangerous. We must take heed lest satisfied ambition have brought inward poverty. One thing is sure: His way is the only way of true fulfilment. All that we really seek in the selfish and material things of life is found by seeking His will for us. Our hunger for life and peace is the real root of our desires whatever they may be set upon. That life and peace can only be found in the way of His will.

278

THE LORD'S PRAYER

LIV

(1) ON THE THRESHOLD

"When ye pray, say, Our Father."
LUKE 11 : 2

MANY fine things have been said about the Lord's Prayer. One of the best is a saying of Marcus Dods: "Though we learned it at our mother's knee, its petitions would take a lifetime to give them all their meaning, and an eternity to give them all their answer." The prayer was Christ's answer to a request of the disciples. No one seeing Jesus at prayer could doubt that something real was happening there. So they asked to be taught to pray. That is our biggest need. When we have learned to pray, we shall no longer be troubled by the question whether prayer is answered. For we shall know by experience that it is. But we shall be looking for something more than cut and dried answers. We shall be seeking and knowing God Himself. And He is greater than all His gifts.

Jesus begins by giving us the keynote of prayer. "When ye pray, say, Our Father." The heart that can say "Our Father" has learned the first lesson in prayer. That is where we must begin, or prayer will bring us little, for we will not have established

281

the true contact with God. The start of all prayer is in a true thought of God. All real religion rises from that spring. It is the same with our approach to God as it is with our approaches to our fellows. What we will ask of anyone will depend on what we think of him. There are people from whom we would not dream of asking anything. There are some to whom we would not dream of taking our troubles. We know them to be hard or unsympathetic, and that thought of them holds us back. It stems prayer at its source.

It is the same with our approach to God. Some of the difficulty we have in prayer may lie here. Our thought of God may be incomplete. There are dark shadows on the picture. These may come from false teaching we had in childhood. They may come from looking at God through the blurred windows of some hard or bitter experience. Some shadows may come from the stains of guilt or shame that darken our conscience and are projected on the face of God. A picture thrown on the screen may have lines or blotches on it that are not in the picture itself. They come from the lantern glass through which the light is thrown. And the whole picture is marred or dim. Our thought of God may be distorted by something in ourselves.

There is only one place to look for the picture of God. It is in the face of Jesus Christ. Some of us forget that the New Testament comes after the

Old, and without the New the Old is incomplete. "All the time," says Struthers, of Greenock, "God was just wearying to show them Jesus." He longed to show us Jesus because He wanted us to know Himself. For through the ages He has been "the great Misunderstood."

The central light of that picture of God is never dim. God is longing to give. That is His kind of love. He is Father. He is like every true father at his best, and better than the best of us. We have our points of selfishness, yet we long to give our children all that is best. How much more God the Father! Christ bids us rest on that, and trust it all the way.

God's father-love is infinitely wise. He will not give us what would in the end destroy or disable us. But there are blessings that can only come with the burdens and purifying that can only come through pain. Some of the things He gives may look very doubtful, but we need not fear to take them from His hands.

This love of His is an individual thing. His care is for each of us, one by one. Jesus strove to make that clear. He knew how our hearts sometimes sink within us when we think of the masses and masses of people round us. How can God single us out? We get a lost and lonely feeling. But it is just the lost and lonely people that God searches out. Maybe we realize our loneliness just that He

283

might find us. "How think ye if a man lose one sheep, if a woman lose one piece of silver, if a man lose one son?" It is always the "one" that matters. That is the kind of father God is.

This father-love of God flames into blazing reality in the Cross. There was nothing sentimental about it. The Cross proves that. Nothing can be so numbing to the spirit as excruciating pain. But even through all the horror and cruelty that gathered round him, Christ saw God's perfect love. He hailed God there as Father. And what he saw amid the clouds and darkness his own heart mirrored in a love for men that is the miracle of history. The first step, then, is to let Christ speak to us of God, and to listen to no other voice. It is to let that love sink in till it conquers all the fear and the fret, and our hearts leap up to say "Our Father."

That is the root of all confidence in prayer. It is not hard to talk to the Father about everything. We can tell Him of our troubles, of the sick child at home, of the lad at school or college about whom we are anxious. We can tell Him of our need for bread, of the hard struggle to make ends meet. We can tell Him of our doubts. We can confess how hard we find it sometimes to trust Him, and how difficult it is to pray. For He knows it all and understands. And what a relief it is to tell Him all the things we often keep to ourselves. We imagine we have to put them right before we can come to Him, when the only way to put them right is just to bring them to Him and open them up to His love.

We can tell Him, too, our struggles; how hard it is to be patient, or to get on with certain people. We can tell Him our sins and weaknesses, the sense of failure and uselessness that comes over us when we see the plague of our own hearts. We need not be afraid. For He knows it all and understands. "If our heart condemn us, God is greater than our heart and knoweth all things."

But it is not *"my* Father" Christ bids us say. It is *"our* Father." We have to get that clear. We shall not ask for things that mean the hurt of others. As we realize His fatherhood, the family feeling comes to us. We begin to include others. The people we do not like, the people we are anxious about, the people who do not know Him, are all His children. He is their Father too. Resentment and prejudice begin to die in that atmosphere of home. For the world begins to have the feel of home when we call God "Father." Our hearts grow tender. Our vision widens until—

> The whole round earth is everywhere
> Bound by gold chains about the feet of God.

LV

(2) HALLOWING THE NAME

"Hallowed be thy name."
LUKE 11: 2

CHRIST always puts first things first. And the first petition in the Lord's Prayer is that God's Name may be hallowed. Real prayer is the focus-point of the deepest desires of our lives. The meaning of this petition is that our first desire must be for God's glory. It is not easy when our hearts are throbbing with the pain of some sharp need to seek God's glory. But His glory is the secret of our own best good. The quickest way out of the Slough of Despond or the prison of selfish care is just to seek that His love and His purpose may be exalted in our lives. When God takes first place in our desire and our reverence, the things that fret and fray our spirits lose their power and the calm of His peace is restored.

The meaning of this petition becomes clear when we think of the Name which Christ has just given to God: "Our Father." It is this Name which is to be hallowed. Nothing is to be allowed to desecrate for us God's name of Father. For there are things that constantly threaten it.

286

We are tempted sometimes, for instance, to think of God as a kind of fate—a soulless force. Thomas Hardy closes the tragic story of Tess with these words: "The President of the Immortals had finished his sport with Tess." That is how he thought of God. The same temptation may come to us. It is strange how the belief in luck or chance still haunts our minds. There are Christian people who will still not sit down to dinner in a party of thirteen. It gives some of us a queer feeling, even though we do not allow the superstition to influence us. We do not think it out, of course. But it means that somehow we feel that there is a region where God does not rule, or where His father-love does not carry. It is the outbreak of primitive fear. But to give way to it is the desecration of God's Name. It is the denial of His Fatherhood. We cannot always trace what brings trouble into our life. But we can be sure that there is order in the process. If we could trace it all out we could see the chain of cause and effect that brought the misfortune. We would find that the end of that chain is held in the strong, wise hands of Almighty Love.

Again, God's name of Father is often threatened by the feeling that He is a taskmaster. Burdens fall and duties are laid on us one by one. Sometimes they seem more than we can bear. There is no escape from the necessity of carrying our load. But at times we resent it. We would like to throw it off.

We cannot see why our load should be so heavy, and that of others so light. We grow sullen and peevish, and life becomes a dreary round without purpose or meaning. We have forgotten that behind it there is a Father who calls us to a service in which He works with us for a plan that is worth while. Christ had a special message for the weary and heavy-laden. He did not come to lift that burden from our shoulders. He came to take the sense of strain and friction from our hearts. "Take my yoke," he said, and a yoke is meant for two. It is a yoke that he shares with us. Duty may be a chain. But it is a golden chain, for it binds us to him. And in time we shall learn to thank him that he gave us the privilege. Even the wash-tub or the bench can be the place of living fellowship with him.

But suffering and sorrow can darken His face for us, and desecrate his Name if we let them. It is so easy to blame God for it all, and to carry in our hearts the feeling of bitterness or resentment. Why should this happen to us? Something must be wrong with the world, and God has been unfair. So we talk to ourselves. And into our hearts comes the dark shadow of enmity toward God. We forget that one of the real qualities of faith is just loyalty. Loyalty is part of all friendship, even with our fellows. If misunderstanding comes, or a friend does something which seems unfriendly, we must at least be loyal. We must believe that there is some misunderstanding. We must give our friend the benefit of the doubt. No friendship can last without this loyalty. And loyalty is also the very heart of faith. If we cannot understand, we can at least trust the Father. And it is better to trust than to understand. The world in which we live is like a house in the building. The scaffolding surrounds it, hiding its growing beauty. The dust of labor shrouds it. The walls look half a ruin. How can order and beauty ever come out of it? So we might ask. But the architect has his plan. Give him time and one day we shall see and be satisfied.

For some of us also the thought of God's Fatherhood may be threatened by the shadows that conscience brings. We have done what we know we should not have done. And the sense of guilt falls on us darkening everything. It seems as if God were standing over us demanding an ideal we cannot reach and yet from which we cannot escape. There is something very real in this experience. It is wrong to try to brush away this feeling of guilt as something morbid. In *The Scarlet Letter* we have the picture of a man who is in the grip of guilt. But in his tormented spirit he knew that he dared not try to banish it. For had he done so, he realized that he would have passed into an unreal world. The sense of guilt is the shadow cast upon us by the purity and holiness of God. But behind it there is the Father's love. He refuses to let us fall below our best. Amid the shadows of guilt that darken His face He is still the Father calling us to live with Him in a world of goodness in which He is able to give us power to live, and which He is bidding us enter through His forgiveness. He is calling us to become in a new way His children.

The people of the Bible believed that there was power in a name. If they knew a man's name, they felt that they had some hold over him. However this may be, to know God's name and hold it fast is to give Him power over us. It is to keep open through everything a road for His grace and love. For God makes Himself known to those who trust Him. To hold on to this is the key to victory. Whatever life may be doing to us we have our hands on the secret of peace and power, if through everything we look to Him and say "Our Father."

LVI

(3) THE RULE OF THE FATHER

"Thy kingdom come."
LUKE 11: 2

WHEN we know God as Father it is natural that we should want His Kingdom to come. The world's need is that He who is Father should rule. At the moment it is like a home without the authority of the father. It is a family without the family spirit. Our very closeness to one another is our danger. We have the power to hurt one another terribly, but not the love to help one another deeply. If only God would rule! That is what it means for His Kingdom to come.

Why does He not rule? It seems so simple when He has the power. If we had the power, we would use it. So we often think. The world seems to have a craving for some strong hand to take the tiller of their lives and steer them. In some countries men who have been able to get the power have seized it, and the people have submitted or even welcomed them in a kind of despair. There is an opportunity in the world today for dictators. Many are willing to give up their freedom in order to be ruled. The burden of ordering their own lives seems to be too heavy. The world is too big for us to manage by our own wisdom. Why does not God rule in this compelling way? He has the power and the wisdom and the love. Why does not He take the throne and rule?

We must, however, be clear in our minds about the method of God's rule: He is not merely King, He is Father. We are not His slaves or His subjects, but His children. It would be easy for Him to compel us to do His will. It would be easy for Him to make us submit to His command. But by that compulsion we should lose our freedom We should be His slaves, not his children. Love cannot compel. It can only win our loyalty. The will cannot be forced, though we may have to submit. The will can only be yielded to one whom we love and to a rule that we see and desire as right and good. It is a long process for God to win this surrender of our hearts. The victory of God is by a long, hard road. It is the road to Calvary, and Jesus went that way, that through His suffering, God's love might win its victory. It is the only way by which the rule of the Father can come.

When we pray this prayer we ought to picture what God's rule would mean. We need imagination in our religion and in our prayers. The best things in the world have come because people used their imagination. What they saw kindled their desire and set them to work. When Livingstone tramped the

292

wilderness and the jungle of Africa he saw something more than the disease and cruelty around him. That alone would have taken the heart out of him. He saw Africa changed, the slave-trade gone. He saw her set free and at the feet of Christ. The thought of what God's Kingdom would mean if it came on earth will make us long for it in a new way. It would mean peace among the nations. The spirit of brotherhood would come. The slums would be banished. Strife and oppression would cease. Imagine the world become a home and all in it a family. Who would not long for it?

The only way in which wrong things can be put right is by God's rule of love becoming effective. For us who believe in Christ there is no other way. The root of evil runs deep. And its real cure must be as deep as the disease. When we think of all that needs to be changed it is so easy to fall into despair, and to feel our helplessness. But it is good to remember that God's favorite place of operation is the region of the impossible. And where we are powerless He works if we give Him opportunity. Our prayer is God's opportunity. Do we really pray definitely and with our hearts for the coming of God's rule? Do we think of this one and that; of the people who lead and who carry responsibility? We criticize them. Do we pray for them? If we did, it may be that God's love would be heard knocking at some doors that seem hopelessly closed. And where that knock is heard, some day the handle will be turned to let Him in.

But there is something more that we can do. God's way into any place in which we are, is through us. That is where our responsibility lies. Our business, for instance, is part of the world we are asking the Father to rule. What of His Kingdom there? What of working with others in the family spirit? Or what of our home? That can be a little bit of the Kingdom of God. In many homes there is love, but it does not rule. Our wills clash. There is conflict of temperaments. So we often call it. There are unconfessed resentments. Home ought to be the unit of God's Kingdom. In it the life of the Kingdom should be found and practiced. Love has the opportunity there to be at its best, and we can know what it fully means. There are two readings of the saying of Christ about lighting a candle. One is that it may give light to all that are in the house. A real religion will begin its penetrating work in the home. The other is that it may give light to all that come into the house. It will reach the outsider through the home into which he comes.

But the Kingdom begins with ourselves. Our heart is a world in itself. God's rule must begin there. "The kingdom of God is within you." It was because the first Christians knew that inner victory of God's love that they could preach to the world. Because of what God had done in their own hearts they had hope and vision for the world without. This prayer is not a reality unless we are offering God the throne within. Years ago a young man who went to the front sent his mother his keys. In a letter he told her, "I am giving you the keys of all my drawers, every one." Praying for God's Kingdom means giving Him all the keys—the power to open every door within. Then comes peace. When we have the peace of God's rule within, His Kingdom comes in us and we know there is power in that love to bring all men in.

LVII

(4) DOING GOD'S WILL

*"Thy will be done, as
in heaven, so in earth."*
LUKE 11 : 2

MOST people when the will of God is mentioned feel
a cold shadow creeping over them. The will of God
has been so often applied to the misfortunes of life.
If a thing is hard it must be the will of God, and we
have just got to submit. So some people think.
And when sorrow or sickness comes, they try to
say, "Thy will be done."

Of course one can understand the comfort of it.
It is a great solace when we have lost a beloved
child to feel that God willed it. It is a comfort when
some accident or misfortune strikes us to feel that
God somehow sent it. It delivers us from the soulless hand of fate. It is a real help to feel that it happened because God knows best. Some fine souls
have found healing and peace in that faith.

But this belief is not easy to hold if we begin to
ask questions. And it has not always been good
for people to hold it, for it has sometimes made
them resigned to evils which they should have opposed. If God sends disease, why try to cure it?

296

If misfortunes are sent by God to try us, why should we always do our best to avoid them?

Some have gone to the other extreme. They have said that God has nothing to do with our sickness or sorrow. But can this be so? He is Father, and things ought not to go on in the home that are out of the control of His wisdom and love. And we cannot believe that they do. There is no part of the jungle of life which He cannot control for His purposes. Jesus has shown us how this control can be exercised. There is a way of facing things by which God can co-operate with us to use them for our good. He has shown us that way. He has blazed the trail through the jungle of pain, and when we catch His Spirit we can meet the trouble so that it becomes a blessing. Sickness is not the deliberate act of God, but Christ's way of meeting it is the way of God's will. That is what we ought to mean when in trouble we pray "Thy will be done."

But there are beautiful things in the will of God. Since God is Father, His will must include all that is good. God's will means health, for instance. He wants disease to be conquered. It must be His will that His children should be fed and cared for where they cannot provide for themselves. The slums of our cities cannot be the will of the Father. He would not have such rooms and cellars in His house. He has put us in the world to make it a

297

home for all His children. It is His will that we
should get to work to clean it up. It cannot be His
will that we should fill the rooms of His house with
deadly explosives and weapons of war with which to
kill each other. We may have to restrain some from
harming themselves and the rest of the family. But
it cannot be His will that we should hate and fear and
kill each other. Doing His will means creating fellowship and peace.

We should think of God's will in this positive
way. All the things that make for a better world
are the will of God for us. It is time we saw it in
that light. This prayer should not be a moan of
resignation. It should be a song set to joyful music.
Why should we always identify the will of God with
something unpleasant? Some of us have an idea
that if there are two roads open and one of them is
hard and disagreeable, that one must be the will of
God. It is good, of course, to keep the balance on
that side. We are so apt to choose the pleasant way
just because it is easy. But it does not always follow
that the unpleasant thing is the right thing.

Some of the misunderstanding may have come
from leaving out the last clause of the prayer, "as
in heaven, so in earth." What could Christ mean
by that? He means that we should do His will joy-
fully and from the heart. There must be no sullen-
ness and no resentment. Love must be the motive.
If we love people enough, it is a joy to do what

they want done. We have not really seen the Father as He is until we can say, "I delight to do Thy will, O my God." We may need to learn that God's will is best by taking our own way and finding it stupid and foolish. Sometimes we can learn in no other way. But we must seek to have Him kindle in us that love to Him which makes His way clear to us and also makes obedience to it a joy. The place where self-will is cast out and God's will becomes first is at the Cross. There the hard core of self will be melted by love, till doing what God wants done is a joy.

But in heaven surely God's will is done with perfect knowledge. How can we know what is God's will? It is one thing to be ready to do it. It is another thing to be clear about what God wants us to do. Many sad mistakes have been made by people who imagined they were doing God's will. We sometimes speak as if conscience were the voice of God. But it is only the medium of His voice. It is like a wireless receiver taking silent messages and making them audible. But our conscience may not be a very good receiver. The messages may be distorted. Conscience may be dull or insensitive. It needs education. The only way is to be constantly open to Christ and to his Spirit as we find him in the Gospels. It is to learn from him. One of R. L. Stevenson's stories was left unfinished, and the last chapters were added after his death by another

299

writer. The latter has told us how he was able to do it in the same style. He had to know Stevenson's mind, to understand the plan of his book, to catch his spirit; so for months he read nothing but Stevenson, till he caught his style. We shall know God's will and do it naturally and simply as we live close enough to Christ to have his mind and be possessed by his purpose. To become daily more sensitive to God's will is the inner meaning of prayer.

LVIII

(5) OUR DAILY BREAD

"Give us this day our daily bread."
LUKE 11 : 3

IT seems a descent to come from praying about God's will to asking for daily bread. Some writers have suggested that Christ meant the bread of the Spirit, but he was talking to simple people who were very conscious of the need of bread. Hunger is the strongest of our appetites. The need of bread makes life a constant struggle. It has created revolutions and riots, and even wars. It is the root of much of our anxiety and worry. We cannot help bringing our need for bread into our prayers if we are honest, for "Prayer is the soul's sincere desire." A good part of our time must be given to thinking and planning about daily bread.

God knows all about this need. He has made us with this hunger. Without it the earth would never have been developed; our best discoveries would never have been made. This need for bread sends us to work day by day, and keeps us at it. And God has provided the supply. Christ bids us look at the flowers and the birds. No artist in dress could produce a garment to outmatch in color and design the garb of the humblest flower. The food of the commonest bird is part of His providing and His infinite care. Most of us live out of touch with nature. Our food comes to us from the factory or the bakery. We are apt to forget that it is all God's gift. The mark of miracle is on every grain of wheat. He knows our physical needs. And so we may bring them to Him. We may come to Him and tell Him everything, our fear about tomorrow, the trouble in the business, the needs of our children. And we may ask Him for daily bread and know that He will help us to get it. The real escape from worry is to take things to Him. "In nothing be anxious," says Paul; "but," he goes on, "in everything by prayer and supplication let your requests be made known unto God." That means telling Him our need for daily bread.

Perhaps we may ask why, since He provides, we need to ask Him. Christ does not mean that prayer should take the place of work. And if we have work that will bring bread, why pray about it?

This hunger of ours, like other instincts, is a mighty force. It has driven people to do desperate things. It can be, like other instincts, a dangerous force if it is not directed aright. There are two ways in which we can use this hunger. We can either make it a merely material thing, and keep it out of our religion and our fellowship with God.

Or we can put it into God's hands, asking Him to direct it and help us to satisfy it rightly. Some people take the first way. They keep religion out of their work and their business. They let the need for bread take hold of them till it becomes feverish greed. They want not only bread for today, which is all Christ bids us ask for, but bread in abundance for tomorrow as well. They crave for security. They fill their barns and build greater, till they have come to settle down in selfish luxury. The struggle for existence can become a very degrading thing.

The right thing to do with this hunger is to open it up to God. That is the way in which it can become safe and right both for ourselves and others. For prayer cleanses it from selfish greed. Prayer takes the bitterness out of the struggle. It takes the strain from the heart. We all need this outlet toward God. Some of us have a hard lot. Work and money are very uncertain. There are the children to be fed. The strain of the struggle is wearing us out. Some of us may be seeking more security than God means us to have. Our life is full of the fear of tomorrow, even though at the moment we have enough. God does not mean us to live like that. He means us to trust Him while we do our best. He bids us make the earning of our bread a partnership with Him. He knows our need, and if we trust Him, the need will be supplied. Strained work is always poor work. "My God shall supply all your

303

need." So Paul wrote from a prison where he had proved it.

But that means that our needs must be simplified. It may be that we shall have to be content with simple things. Perhaps our demands need to be brought to the light of God's standards of efficiency. Jesus put the prayer for doing the will of God and for His Kingdom before that for daily bread. If we pray about material things in this spirit, there are some that we shall cease to ask for. We shall be content to have them or not as God wills. We shall learn the power both to manage plenty and to face poverty.

But the prayer is not "Give me." It is "Give us." The Lord's Prayer is social all through. It is always "us," never "me." And this is most true of the prayer for bread. Christ tells a story of a youth who went into life saying "Give me." And he ended that part of his career alone, and hungry to the point of starvation. We are very slow to learn the lesson. Sharing is the road to possessing. Co-operation is the secret of abundance. The wheels of industry are being slowed up or are standing still because we refuse to co-operate with one another. The selfish spirit can never be the driving power of life without, in the end, causing the machinery to break down. That is the lesson which our present economic distress is bringing home to us. Many are hungry today because the world has not learned it. Christ bids us learn it for ourselves that we may help the world to learn it too. The key which opens the kingdom of earth is found when we are seeking the Kingdom of God. And in this prayer Christ puts it into our hands.

LIX

(6) THE FORGIVENESS OF SINS

"Forgive us our sins."
LUKE 11 : 4

No prayer can be complete without a petition about our sins. Some people object to this constant occupation with our sins. It seems a lack of what they imagine is "healthy-mindedness." But Jesus puts the need of forgiveness alongside of the need of bread. Something is wrong with our body if it is not aware at times of hunger. And something is wrong with the soul if there is not a longing for forgiveness. The sense of sin is one of the signs of a healthy soul.

> They who fain would love Thee best
> Are conscious most of wrong within.

The sense of sin is the greatest lack in the lives of most of us. We are very sensitive in these days to disease. But we do not feel deeply the broken laws, the worry and fear, that are the roots of it. We think a great deal about the slums. Their ugliness and sordidness nauseate us. But we do not feel as we ought the shame of our corporate responsibility for these things. It is the lack of love which really keeps them in being. There are slums in the world because there is a slum in our hearts. We are distressed by the friction and strain that often spoil the sweetness of home. But we do not deeply realize the self-will and pride that lie behind these things. It is sin which is the secret root of all our trouble. The beginning of a new world would be found if we learned to pray the prodigal's prayer—"Father, I have sinned." When he had come to this conviction he had come to himself. He had begun to see things clearly. He had come to know himself. He had taken the first step into a new life.

For what is sin when you get down to it? It is not an act, though it results in various kinds of wrong actions. It is a condition. It is the refusal to live as the children of the Father. It is the rejection of God's fellowship and of life in that fellowship. That refusal may be unconscious. It may come through blindness to the love of God, and to all that love asks of us. Or it may come through definite and deliberate self-will. We want our own way. We hate the hard road of right or duty. We prefer the pleasant meadows of pleasure or pride or self-indulgence. That in itself produces blindness to God's love. The more we disobey, the less we feel the challenge of conscience, the less sensitive we become to the gentle voice within. Sin deadens the heart to all that is best. As Burns put it out of his own experience:

307

It hardens a' within,
And petrifies the feeling.

It was, in part, to awaken the sense of sin that Jesus died. When we see the Cross we see what sin is. It is the kind of thing which makes a world in which the Son of God was not allowed to live. If we only stood long enough before the Cross, we would become aware of things in ourselves and in our lives which would produce the cry for forgiveness.

But what is it we are asking when we pray for forgiveness? It is for nothing less than restoration to God's fellowship. The word "forgiveness" is an inadequate word. Jesus used it because he found it ready to his hand. But he put into it a meaning that made it entirely new. We think of it still as the cancellation of a debt. We owe to God a devotion, a love, which we have refused. In our refusal we have said things and done things which have put blots on the pages of life. And when we ask forgiveness, we ask that He will erase these blots and forget them. We ask that He will not hold them against us. And with that we may be content. But God is not content with that. In point of fact, there are things done which cannot be undone. We cannot recall the ugly word. The broken law may go on registering itself in some weakness of body. It may be that some shameful act of ours has poisoned the life of another who has passed beyond our influence. Our tears cannot wash away the results of it. Some people carry through life the burden and the sorrow of lives which they have hurt, and even the sense of God's forgiveness brings no peace. What does Christ mean by forgiveness?

He really means the restoration to God's fellowship. Nothing less than this is what He offers. And nothing less than this is what Christ bids us ask. His forgiveness means all that it meant in the father's welcome to the returning prodigal. It means the full rights of sonship, with nothing between to cloud the love. He will never hold our sin against us. "Our sins and our iniquities He will remember no more." "As far as the east is from the west, so far hath He removed our transgressions from us." It is as complete as that. To realize this, in itself, is unutterably wonderful. But what is more, He gives us all we need for living the life of His children. We come to Him with our forfeited sonship, in rags and shame. And He takes us to Himself as His children. He gives us the robe of His righteousness, and a ring which is the symbol of the love that never lets go.

But there is something even more. What of the kind of world we have made for ourselves by the things we have done, the mistakes and the selfishness? What of the things that have passed beyond recall and have wrought havoc in the home or the lives of others? There is a glorious answer. He

309

takes responsibility for our whole situation if we put it into His hands. Through His fellowship it can be redeemed, as we let His Spirit direct us. There is nothing with such hope in it as the message of forgiveness. We may not see all the transforming results, but we can leave that burden with Him, and He will carry it.

Only we must be sincere. We must be willing to seek and to claim all that forgiveness means. We must be ready to enter fully into the life of fellowship with the Father in everything. That is what it means to say, "Forgive us our sins."

LX

(7) THE FORGIVING SPIRIT

"Forgive us as we forgive."
LUKE 11 : 4

THESE words put a big strain on our sincerity. As we forgive! But this is the condition that Christ lays down. And it is absolute. There is no escape from it. He told a story to make it clear. It was the story of a man with a debt he could not pay. This debt was canceled by the kindness of the creditor, but the debtor who had been forgiven refused to forgive others a smaller debt which they owed to him. The result was that those who had forgiven him withdrew their kindness and cast him into prison till he should pay his debt to the full. Christ laid down this condition with all the emphasis he could: "If ye will not forgive, neither will your heavenly Father forgive you."

What does it involve? He cannot mean that we can win God's forgiveness of ourselves by our forgiveness of others. For in our relation to God we are in the realm of mercy, not of merit. But our willingness to forgive is the test of our willingness to live as God's children. And it is only when we are willing to come into this new relationship to

God that His forgiveness can become a reality and a power. If we have a resentment or a grudge against another which we are unwilling to give up, we are not yet open to His love. The gates are locked against the entrance of His Spirit into our hearts. His forgiving love cannot get to work in us and for us. Pride or anger is holding the citadel within. Self is still on the throne. Let us think it out.

As we forgive! How deep does our forgiveness go? Let us examine some of our relationships. Here is someone who has wronged us, or has done something of which we strongly disapprove. How deep does our forgiveness go? We hold them at arm's length. Or we treat them with a certain coldness. We may not actually seek to do them an injury, but we do not want to be friends. We find it hard to forget or to be natural and kindly with them. There is always that secret grudge chilling our spirit. We have no great interest in what happens to them. If they get into trouble, we should not feel any great regret. Is that the extent to which we would like God to forgive us? As we forgive! How would it be with us if God stood aloof from us like that in a peevish indifference or sullen resentment?

As we forgive! We must apply this word in relation to others as widely and fully as Christ applies the forgiveness of God. It means for one thing that we must definitely get rid of the resentment or the grudge. "As far as the east is from the west, so

312

far has he removed our transgressions from us." That is the measure of His forgiveness. It is absolute. He lets nothing stand between us and Him. The past is buried. So God forgives. And our forgiveness must mean the same complete reconciliation to our brother in our hearts.

It means even more than that if we are to forgive as God forgives. It means the active desire to restore the other to friendship. We must be willing to come into a new relation with him or her, so that we can help each other. For that is what God's forgiveness means. Nothing less is worth while. Perhaps we say to ourselves by way of excuse that we cannot forgive people till they are ready to be forgiven. How can we forgive till they are ready to tell us that they are sorry and to ask for our pardon? That sounds reasonable. But in many cases it is only an excuse. And it falls short of what God does. For His forgiveness is more than His answer to the cry of our penitence. It is the going forth toward us of His love, to create in us the penitent spirit, and to make us ready to be forgiven. Think of Christ on the Cross. His last cry was the prayer that his enemies might be forgiven. It was the going forth of his forgiving love, seeking to awaken in them the desire for forgiveness. And it worked. It touched the soul of the thief by his side, so that he felt his need, and asked for the gift of that healing love. The spirit of God's children is

313

the spirit that longs to be reconciled to others, and seeks to heal the breach. It is not easy to take this reconciling way. Christ is asking a very hard thing of us. For pride bars the way and forbids. Yet that is the condition on which Christ bids us pray. Only to this forgiving spirit does he promise the forgiveness of God.

We do not always realize how important it is. It may be the crucial point in a vital experience of Christ. There are various kinds of barriers that keep him out of our lives, and when we come to take him seriously we find them out. The most common barrier is in our relationship with others. There is a cold hard bit of pride lurking in us. And the test of our willingness to let Christ into our life is our willingness to let these things go. It may mean taking some step which will humiliate us. It is not easy to get rid of a long-cherished grievance. It may help us to do it if we realize that a wrong or bitter spirit is a heavy load to carry. Hate and antagonism may sometimes seem to give us a subtle pleasure. But a wrong spirit always brings unhappiness to ourselves. It is a kind of bondage. When land is being brought under cultivation, there are sour places that have to be drained. Hatred is a kind of swamp in the mind breeding poison.

It may help us also if we remember that it is through our human love that God gets into the lives of others. Some people can only realize the for-

314

giveness of God through the forgiveness of their fellows. A man who recently found Christ tells how he first felt the love of God through the wonderful forgiveness of some people whom he met. He had been half afraid to meet them lest they should despise him and make him feel an outcast. But when they accepted him as a brother without any trace of blame or coldness, the wonderful light of God's forgiving love broke in. It may be there are some around us who are waiting to find God's love through our forgiveness of them.

But if we are willing, Christ can take away the resentment and the bitterness. A little time of waiting in spirit before the Cross will help to cleanse it away. We will become so conscious of our own weakness that we will have nothing but pity for the weaknesses of others. We may not be able to see their sins when we have seen our own. Pride will be broken, so that his love can come into our hearts. And in that love, other people will become lovable. We shall become weary of strife and misunderstanding, and filled with the longing to reconcile. It may mean taking the way of the Cross to do it, and accepting suffering and misunderstanding and humiliation. But that is the authentic road. Our forgiveness cost him all that and more.

> It is the way the Master went.
> Shall not the servant tread it still?

LXI

(8) OUT OF TEMPTATION

"Lead us not into temptation."
MATT. 6: 13

THIS is a difficult prayer to pray. It is not because it is hard to ask, but because it is difficult to understand. We have been taught to think that temptation is a useful thing. It is a prelude to sin, indeed, for it is through temptation that sin enters our life. But we know that without temptation no man could win character. Temptation is a form of choice. It is the choice between the evil and the good. Life makes to us various kinds of appeal. It appeals to our pride, to greed, to fear on the one hand. And it appeals to our unselfishness, to our love for others, to our courage. We are constantly aware, if we are living seriously, of a conflict of choices. And the lower choice is what we call a temptation. Without this conflict and the victory over temptation which we can win, we would become flabby. Life would just be drifting with the stream. We would not develop strength of character. The growth of personality comes through conflict and victory. "No man has been through the university of life till he has been well tempted." Even Christ had his tempta-

tions. He must have told the story of them himself
He had to go into the desert to think out his methods and make his choice of the road he was to follow.
And the choice faced him in three different ways,
so we are told. In all three he overcame the temptation to take the lower way. His soul was stronger
and his mind clearer through that victory. It helped
him later on when he had to meet these same temptations in the actual circumstances of life. Even the
last steps on the way to Calvary were preceded by
the struggle in Gethsemane. Here, then, is our difficulty. If temptation is useful and inevitable, how can
we ask God not to lead us into it?

The difficulty has been met by a new translation
of these words which reads, "Let us not yield to
temptation." But if we think deeply we may feel
that that reading misses something. The ordinary
reading is a prayer for God's leading. It is the only
petition for guidance which the Lord's Prayer con-
tains. Can we not think of circumstances in which
we might want to pray that God would so lead us
that we should not fall into temptation?

For one thing, it is surely wrong to take needless
risks. It is a perilous thing to play with evil. Most
of us are very prone to seek for things in life which
would bring us into moral peril without considering
the risks we run. If duty calls, it is right to take
risks. But if we are merely seeking pleasure or enjoyment, it is another matter. A man may ply his

boat in the waters above the cataract without danger if he keep at a certain distance from the falls. He may make pleasure excursions and be unharmed, but there is a point beyond which the grip of the current will be too strong for him. He would be a fool to risk it except in an emergency of need or duty. It is the same with ourselves. There are situations in which we have no right to take moral risks. We are not here just to enjoy ourselves or to taste experiences. We are here to do the will of God and to seek His Kingdom. Christ said many hard things which had sound sense behind them. "If thine eye or thy foot offend thee, cut them off, and cast them from thee." No experience is worth enjoying at the peril of our souls. Friendship and pleasure are the gifts of God. But if in seeking these we must expose ourselves to a big temptation, there is just one thing to do. It is to avoid them. It is for this kind of leading that Christ bids us pray. There is a sensitive plant whose leaves curl up at every threat of injury. Christ bids us pray for such sensitiveness to evil that we shall become aware of danger and avoid it.

But there is something deeper. The more we become attuned to His will the less some things will tempt us. His hope for us is that we may come to a point of vitality where certain things will cease to tempt us. Their appeal will fall on deaf ears. He said of himself, after the last victory, "The prince of this world cometh and hath nothing in me." There is such a thing in our physical nature as the power of resisting disease. We have to live in the world as we find it. In certain cases it may be possible to make our dwelling among clean mountain air and keep our health. For most of us this is not possible. What we have to do is to gain and keep the physical vitality which can overcome the germs of disease. It is that kind of resisting power which Christ would have us win.

We find it as we are led more deeply into His fellowship. We escape temptation in the right way by allowing ourselves to be guided by God. If our way is chosen at the bidding of caprice and selfishness, we shall meet with temptation, and shall not be able to resist it. But if our first desire is that God should guide, if we are seeking His Kingdom all the time, everything will be changed. New interests will awaken. Pride and fear and greed will die. We shall become conscious of the things that appeal to our true selves. More and more the best things in life will have power over us. We shall become enriched by the world without being ensnared by it. Even in situations that once were full of temptation, we shall be only aware of God's call to us.

The road of life we have to walk may be full of what might be temptation. God will not take us out of the world in order to save our souls. Are we in some place that is difficult? It may be God needs us

319

there. But if we are there with Him and are following His guiding, we shall be more conscious of Him than we are of anything else. We shall fear no evil, for He is with us. "With the temptation He will provide a way of escape"—the shelter of His love, the shadow of Christ's Cross.

LXII

(9) DELIVERANCE FROM EVIL

"Deliver us from evil."
MATT. 6: 13

THIS is the last petition in the Lord's Prayer; it strikes a note of hope. God does not bid us ask for anything He does not mean to give. And deliverance from evil is one of the gifts He has in keeping for us, till we are ready to claim it.

This is where most of us fail. Have we ever realized that victory over evil is possible and assured? God does not promise that we shall be kept from misfortune. Sorrow and trouble may invade our life. They are part of our human burden. And Christ bore it himself to encourage us bravely to take our share. But God does promise that nothing that happens to us need bring us into moral defeat. Have we ever realized this? Have we claimed the fullness of his promised victory? Are there not things in our life with which we compromise because we do not really believe we can be free? John puts it very boldly: "He that is born of God doth not commit sin." Whatever may be tripping us up in the home, in our relationships with others, need not remain to baffle us. Christ meant us to claim the victory when he bade us pray for deliverance.

How this victory comes we do not need to understand. Countless people have found freedom just by claiming it. But it does help if we can see the way. The essential thing is that prayer brings us into a new climate. A man may struggle for life in a poisonous atmosphere, but the struggle will only exhaust him and increase his weakness. What he needs is an open window which will admit a stream of fresh air. Real prayer is like that. It is opening a window to let in a new atmosphere. It redirects our minds. It fixes our attention upon God and His power. And that is the secret of victory. It opens God's way into our lives. It brings us into the clean, vitalizing air of His Presence. "The fear of the Lord is clean," said the Psalmist.

The first effect of that new climate is that we begin to see sin for what it is and thereby its grip is slackened. A good many things have power over us because we call them by soft or attractive names. We are irritable at home, for instance. We call it tiredness. We say we are highly strung. Christ calls it sin. We are easy and self-indulgent with ourselves. We make excuses for it. Christ calls it sin. We are offended with certain people. We nurse resentments or carry our heads high. We call it legitimate pride. Christ calls it sin. The moment we really face up to his standards, we discover what poisonous things we have been harboring in our lives, calling them by names that disguise their true nature. When we are face to face with Christ, we know them for what they are. One night some people came home to find that their house had been burglarized. The thief had taken all he could find. But in the drawing room there was a silver crucifix which remained untouched. He had not dared to take that. And before he could touch anything else he had taken the crucifix and set it with the face to the wall. When Christ is allowed to look in on our life there are things we cannot do because we see them for what they are. In his light they became ugly and repulsive. And that is the first step to deliverance.

But there is more. In this new climate we become conscious of God's love and power. Things we had not realized before to be so lovely begin to shine for us. We see other people in His light. Their faults and follies begin to fall out of the picture. We see them as those whom God loves and whom He enables us to love. We realize the joy and beauty of Christ's kind of life. We discover that sin not only blots the pages of life; it is a waste of energy. It is like steam escaping from an engine. It is like water overflowing from a river, making the meadows stagnant. Christ wants that power. He wants all these instincts, whose force breaks out in shameful and ugly ways, for his Kingdom. And he can take them into his control and use them. Deliverance from evil is not a negative thing. It is the rescue of powers which are going wrong. It is like an orchestra in the hands of a master. The instruments are not silenced. Their music is drawn into the harmony, blended together to make a melody that is rich and full. Christ is that kind of master. Deliverance from evil means having our powers transformed and blended into his kind of life.

We can only have this deliverance on one condition. It is that we are seeking His Kingdom with all our being. This prayer is not a short cut to purity or self-control. Some of us would like that. There are things we would like to get rid of on our own terms. We would like to be free from temper or impurity and the like, and yet be allowed to keep our own selfish way of life. We would like to have life patched and tinkered here and there, or get rid of this bad habit or that, and yet go on as we are living. God never solves our moral problems by cutting knots. It is only as we let Him possess the whole of life that He can renew it. It is only as He is allowed to renew it that He can set us free. What we call a little sin may be like a trifling pain. It may be the symptom of a deep-seated disease. It can only be cured by tackling the disease at the roots.

But our greatest need is to claim this deliverance. It would make a new thing of life if we opened our eyes to the possibility of victory over some things that we tolerate. Suppose we sit down and take a look into our life through the eyes of Christ. We would see things there that have no right to be in those who profess his name. He is waiting to give us deliverance the moment we are ready to take him seriously and claim it. "If we confess our sin, he is faithful and just to forgive us our sin and to cleanse us from all unrighteousness." It is *all* unrighteousness. Nothing less he offers. This is our birthright through his Cross. Can we be satisfied with less than he is willing to give?

LXIII

GOD'S CROWNING MERCY

*"Thou crownest the year
with thy goodness."*
Ps. 65: 11

FOR people on the land, the harvest is the crown
of the year. The long months of sowing and till-
ing have brought them varied experiences. There
has been much labor and many anxieties. Frost
and rain, drought and tempest, have been their lot.
Some days have been happy, and some have been
dreary and hard. But in the harvest God has visited
them. His goodness has banished all their fears
and fulfilled all their hopes. Whatever voices have
whispered to them, the last word is with God, and the
last word is His goodness. "Thou crownest the year
with thy goodness."

There is a message of encouragement here for
us all. To begin with, there is a word for all patient and faithful workers. Good work will have its
reward in the end. It is sometimes hard to believe
this. Many a man has labored long and well, and
very little has come of it. Trouble and misfortune
have dogged his steps. Others who deserved them
less have got the prizes. Some people grow cynical

and tell themselves it is only a matter of luck. But when all is said and done, good work tells. Some day it will bring its reward. It may not be in hard cash and what are called the good things of life; but there are deeper satisfactions. "Something attempted, something done" brings its own content to the heart. Whatever else may come, that must always be the real reward of labor. Good work cannot be done unless that is our chief concern. But there is something more. "All who have meant good work have done good work," says Stevenson. There is a secret book in which the records of labor are kept. Something is being built up by all good work beyond the walls of time. Even our humble toil is treasured up by God for some big purpose of His own. So Kipling sings of the workman who does his job well:

> One stone the more swings to her place
> In that great Temple of Thy worth.

When the man who has used his gifts, whatever they are, comes to give account, God will say, "Well done, thou good and faithful servant: enter thou into the joy of thy Lord." The days may have been hard. The work may have been dreary. There are doubts and discouragements and fears. But the last word will be the goodness of God.

There is a word here, also, for brave and faithful lives. Life itself is in many ways like the farmer's

327

year. There are droughts and storms as well as fair weather. There are cloudy days as well as sunny skies. What is to come out of it all? So we sometimes wonder. Often we have our doubts. There are voices within that tell us that life means nothing and produces nothing. There are voices outside in the world that echo our moods of despair. A ship has at times to sail through rain and mist without a hint of anything ahead. The passengers might be tempted to wonder if they were getting anywhere. But they know the captain is to be trusted. That fact keeps their hearts at rest and gives them patience. So it should be with us in some long and weary bout of sickness or trouble. Our Captain is to be trusted. There is a haven ahead and He will see us through to it. As we grow older, if we are learning from the past, we grow calmer and more patient. Looking back, we see how needless were many of our anxieties. We got through at last, and we knew that the trouble had been worth while. The last word was the goodness of God. This is our comfort also amid our own failures and sin. The big fact, when we are overshadowed by guilt or despair, is the mercy of God. The last word is His goodness.

So it will be when life is over. The last word will not be misfortune or sorrow or defeat. It will be the goodness of God for those who take His way and keep their faith. The 23d Psalm is a mirror of life lived with God. There are varied experiences reflected there. The man who wrote it had seen many kinds of weather. He had known the threat of poverty. He had been through days when his heart failed. He had been tempted at times to leave the track of righteousness. He had known places where life was so dark he could see nothing. He had been encircled with foes. But, all through, God had been with him. At the end of it all, this is his assurance: "Goodness and mercy shall follow me all the days of my life: and I will dwell in the house of the Lord forever." The last word is not doubt or fear or despair or nothingness. The last word will be His goodness.

We need to keep this in mind as we look ahead. The most crushing experience is that of death. It looks terribly final. But death is not the last word. The last word is the goodness of God. It is here that we need to get back to the essential message of Christianity. The old hymns nearly always had a concluding verse about heaven. We moderns are tempted to smile at them. They were often crude or highly colored. But they kept the windows open to the other country. "Now, I further saw," says Bunyan at the end of his story, "that betwixt them and the gate was a river. But there was no bridge to go over and the river was very deep. . . . They addressed themselves to the water, and, entering, Christian began to sink, crying to his brother, 'The billows go over me.' After that a great horror and darkness fell upon him. . . . Then he brake out with a loud voice, 'O, I see Him again.' Thereafter he found ground to stand on, and thus they got over. Then I heard in my dream that all the bells of the City rang for joy." The last word is not the dark river; it is the City of God.

ACKNOWLEDGMENTS

These articles have all appeared in the columns of the *British Weekly*, in which they first appeared, and are reproduced here with but little alteration.

I am under a deep debt of gratitude to Miss Alice Armstrong for her devoted help, and also to Dr. H. E. Lankester, who has very kindly read the proofs.

J. R.